Treasures of the Ocean

Designs to Inspire Your Creative Genius

Published in 2015 by Global Insight Productions

Illustrations by Surabhi
Creative Director Rosa MeChel

www.BeHappyColoringBooks.com

ISBN: 978-0-9970296-2-8

Join Our Creative Community

BeHappyColoringBooks.com

For your coloring and painting pleasure,
if you have creative genius ideas that you
would like for our artist to design, let us know.

We also want you to be a part of our Be Happy
Art Gallery. So go ahead and send us your
masterpiece and we will share it with the world.

You can contact us at **info@behappycoloring.com**

facebook.com/behappycoloring

pinterest.com/behappycoloring

Instagram.com/behappycoloring

twitter.com/behappycoloring

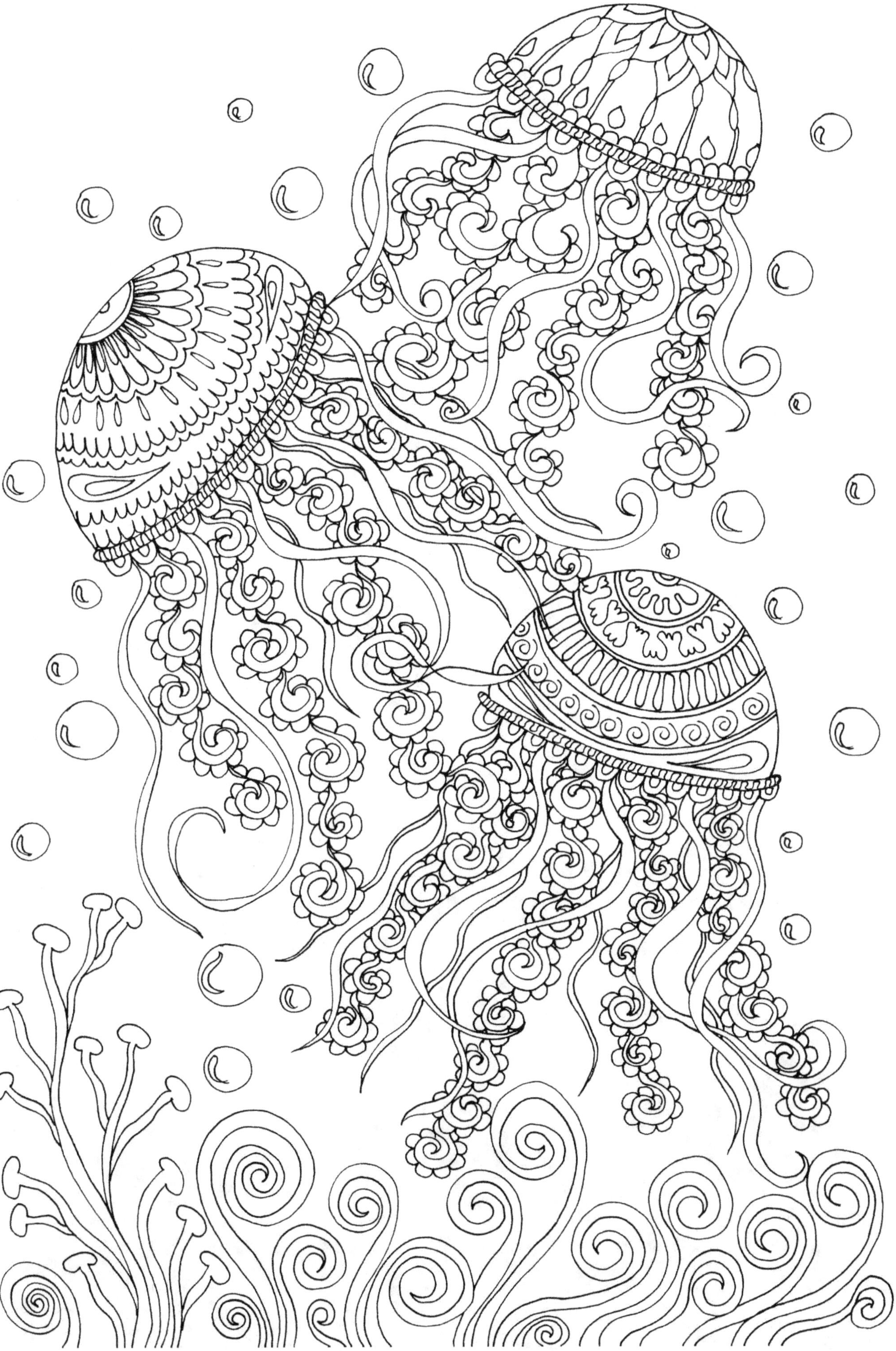

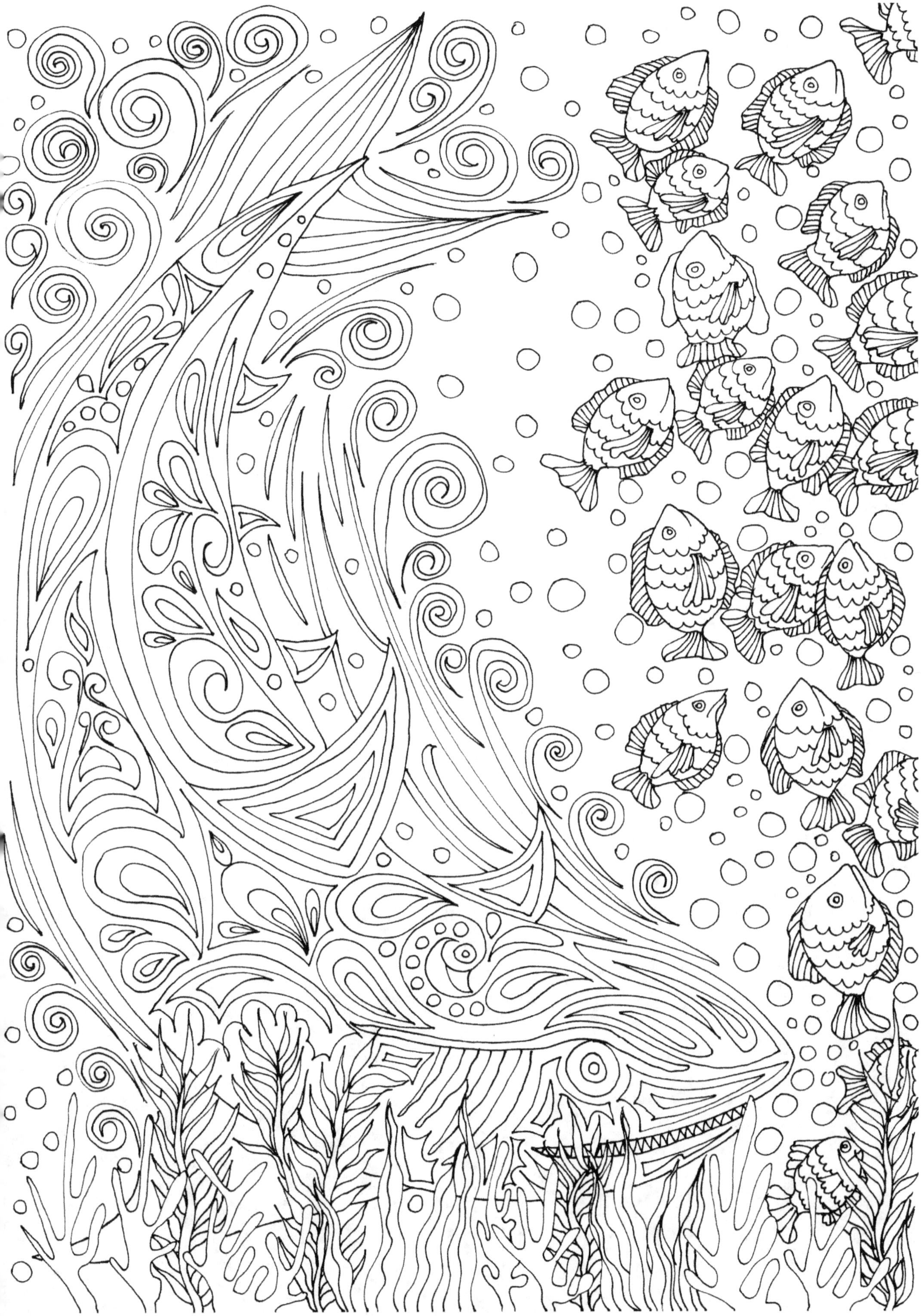

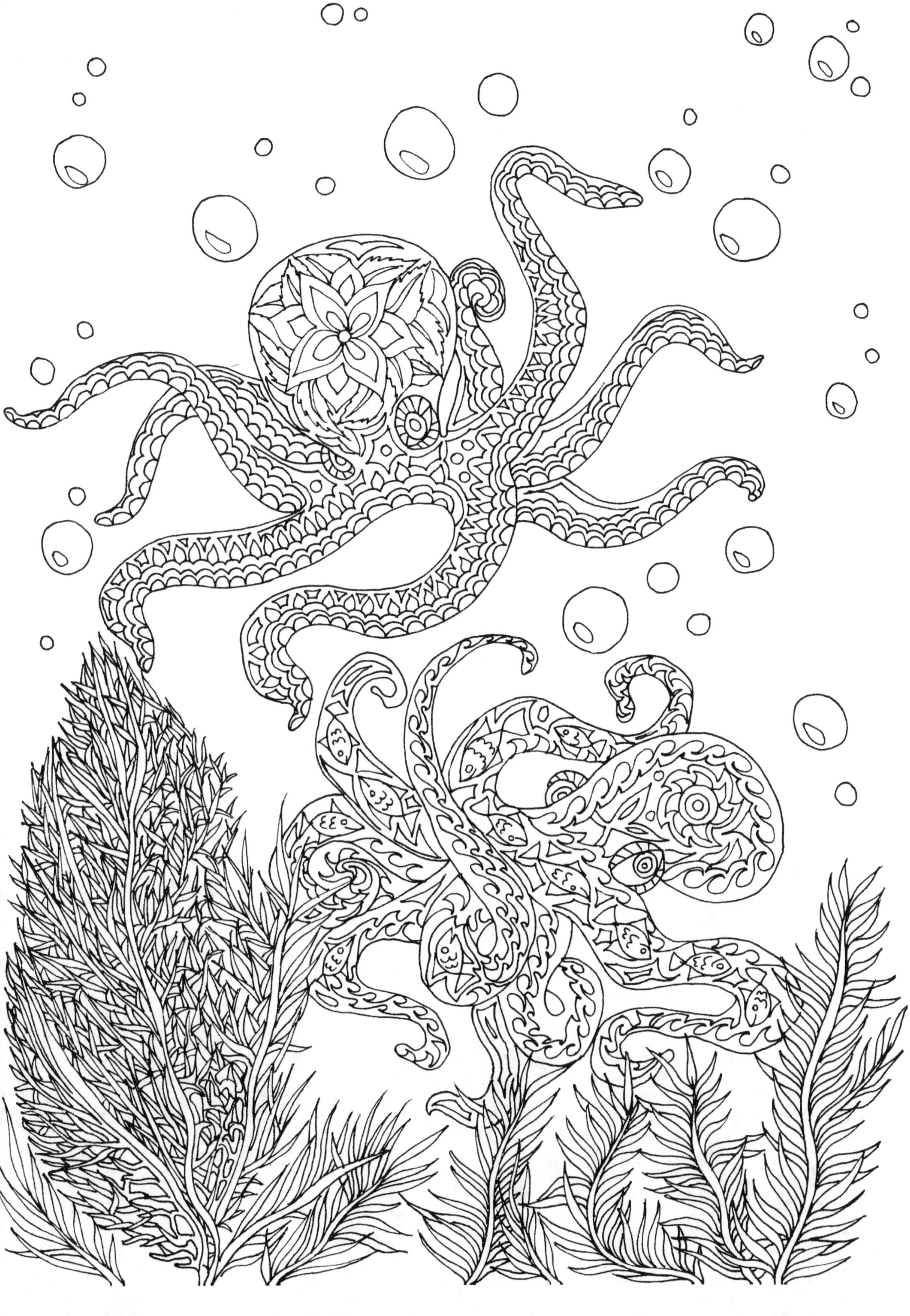

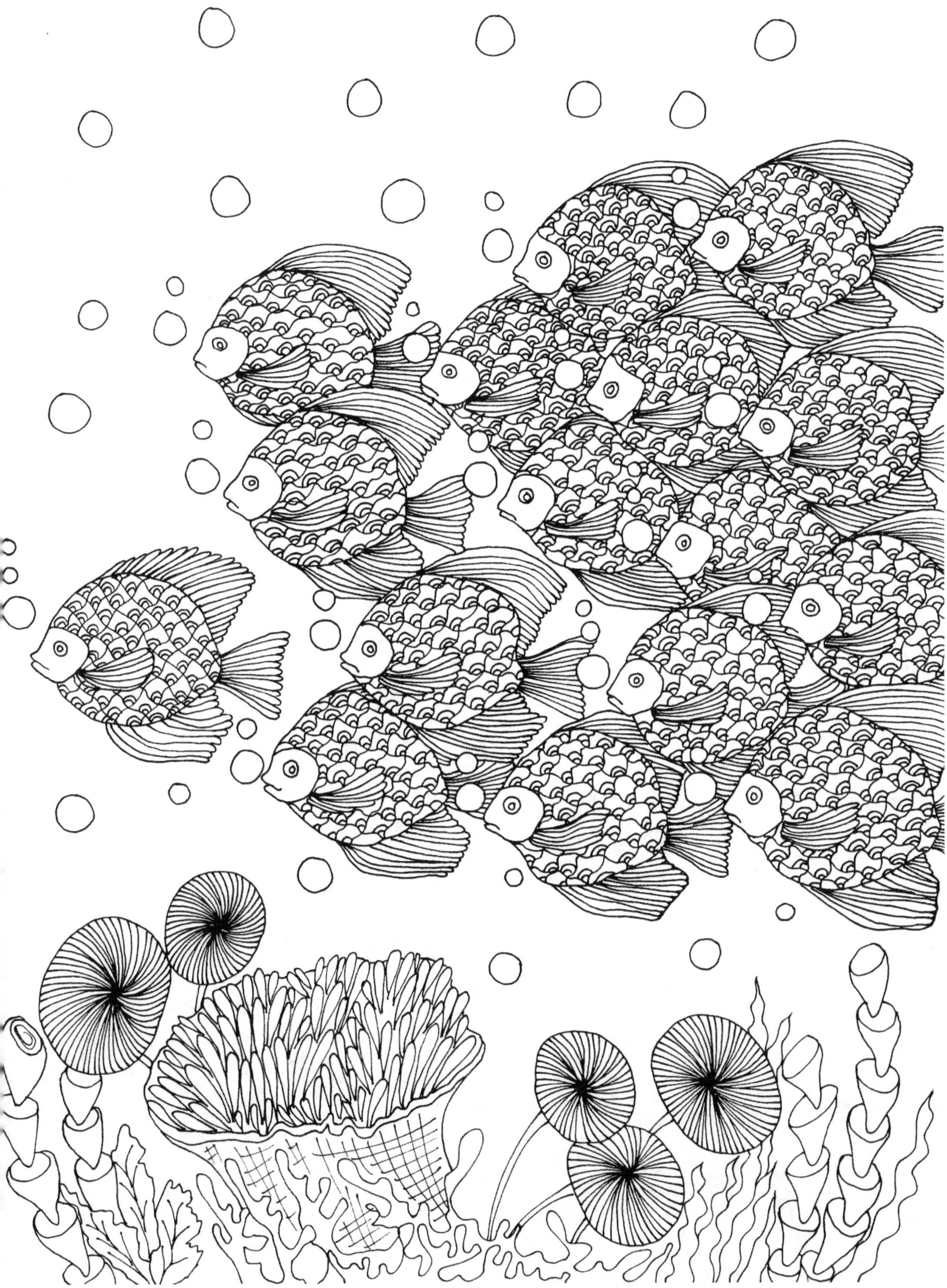

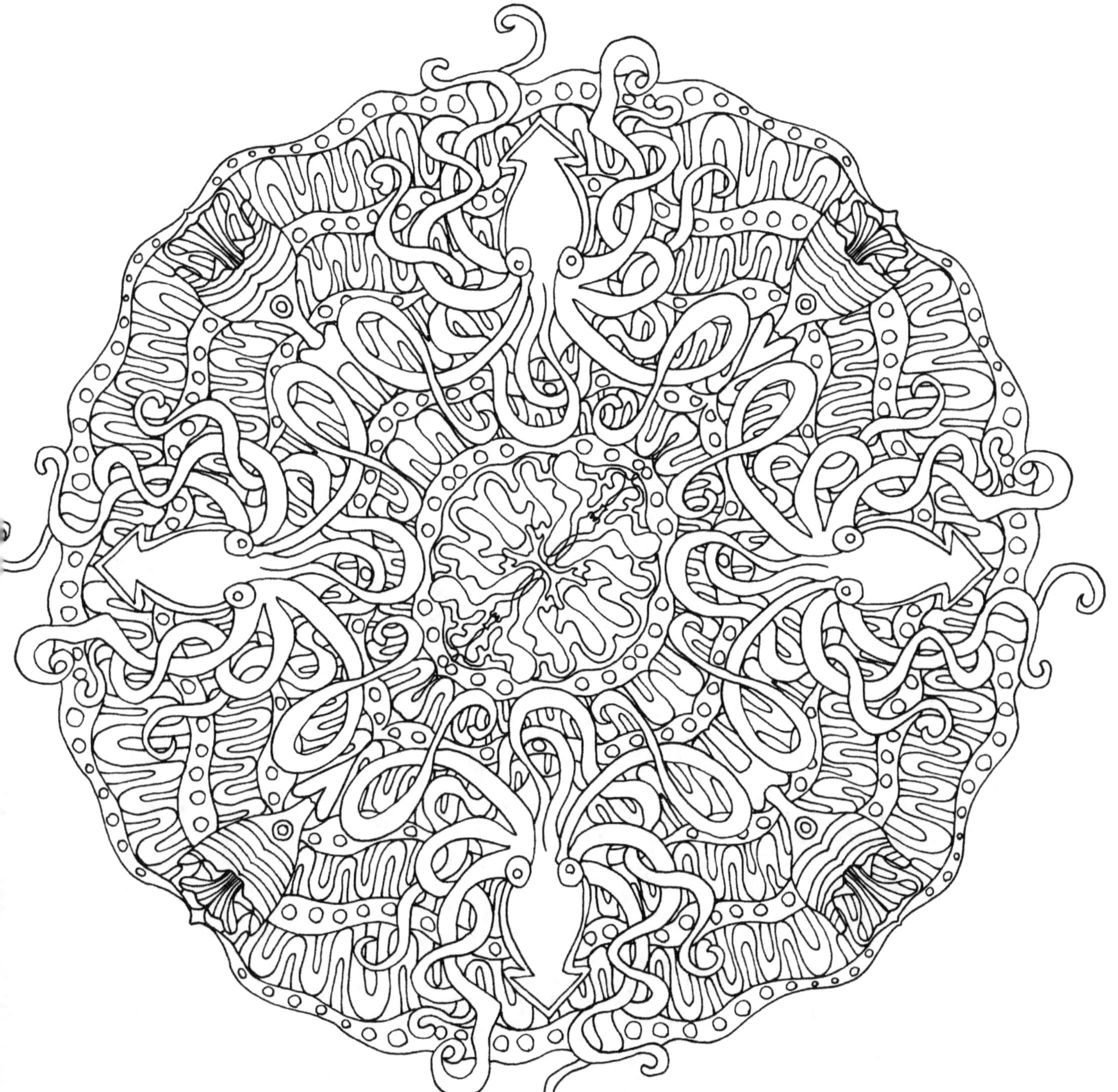

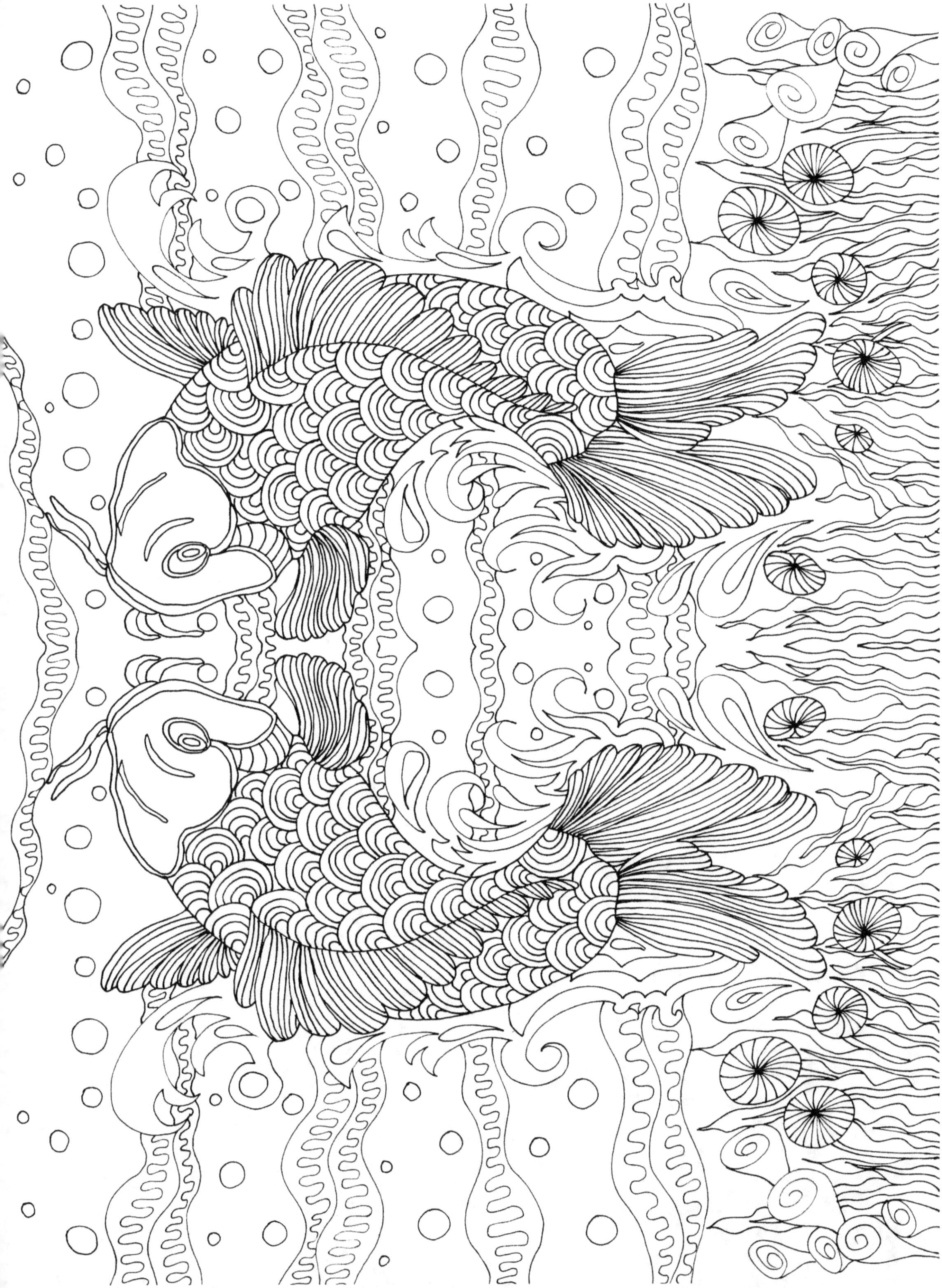

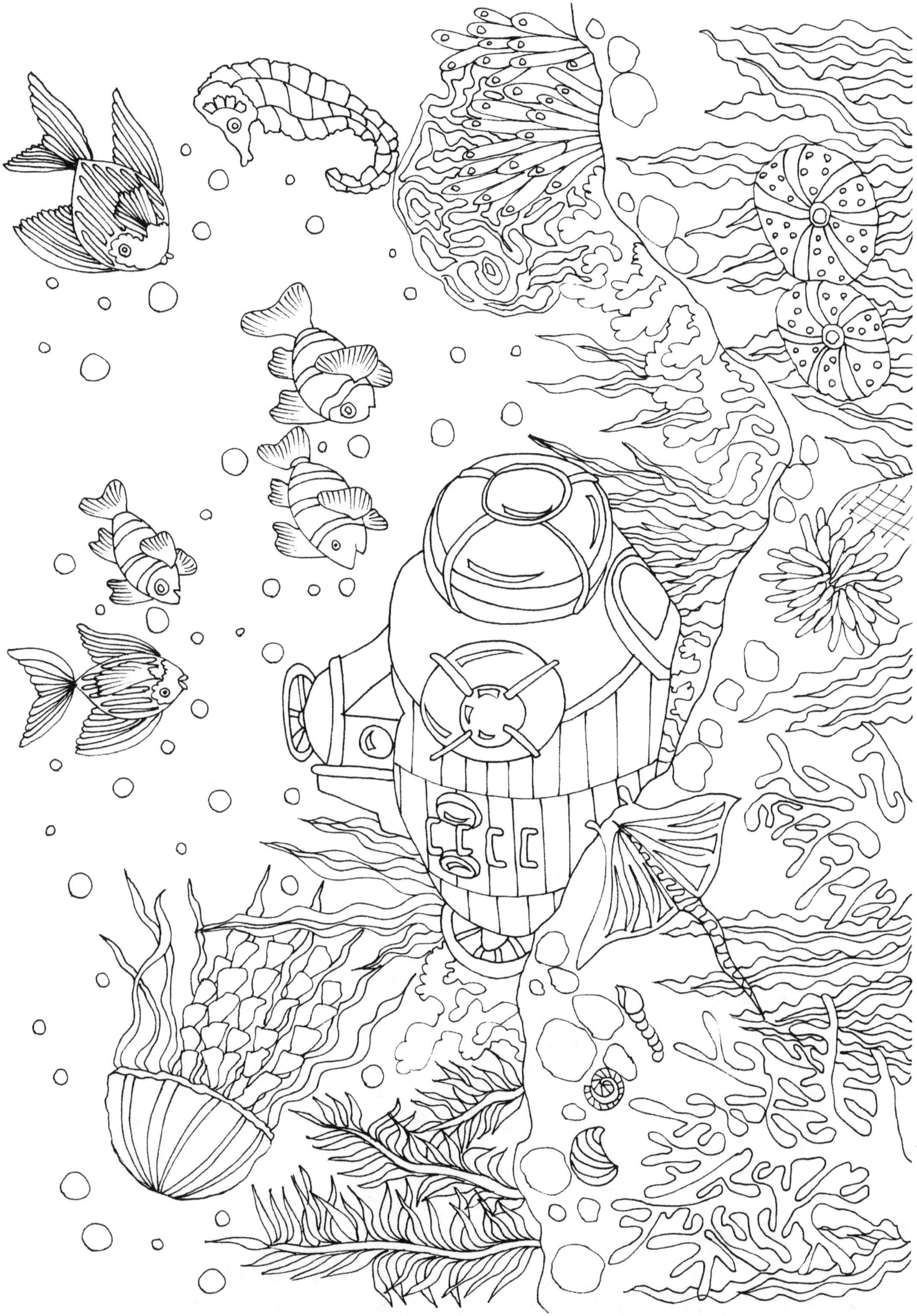

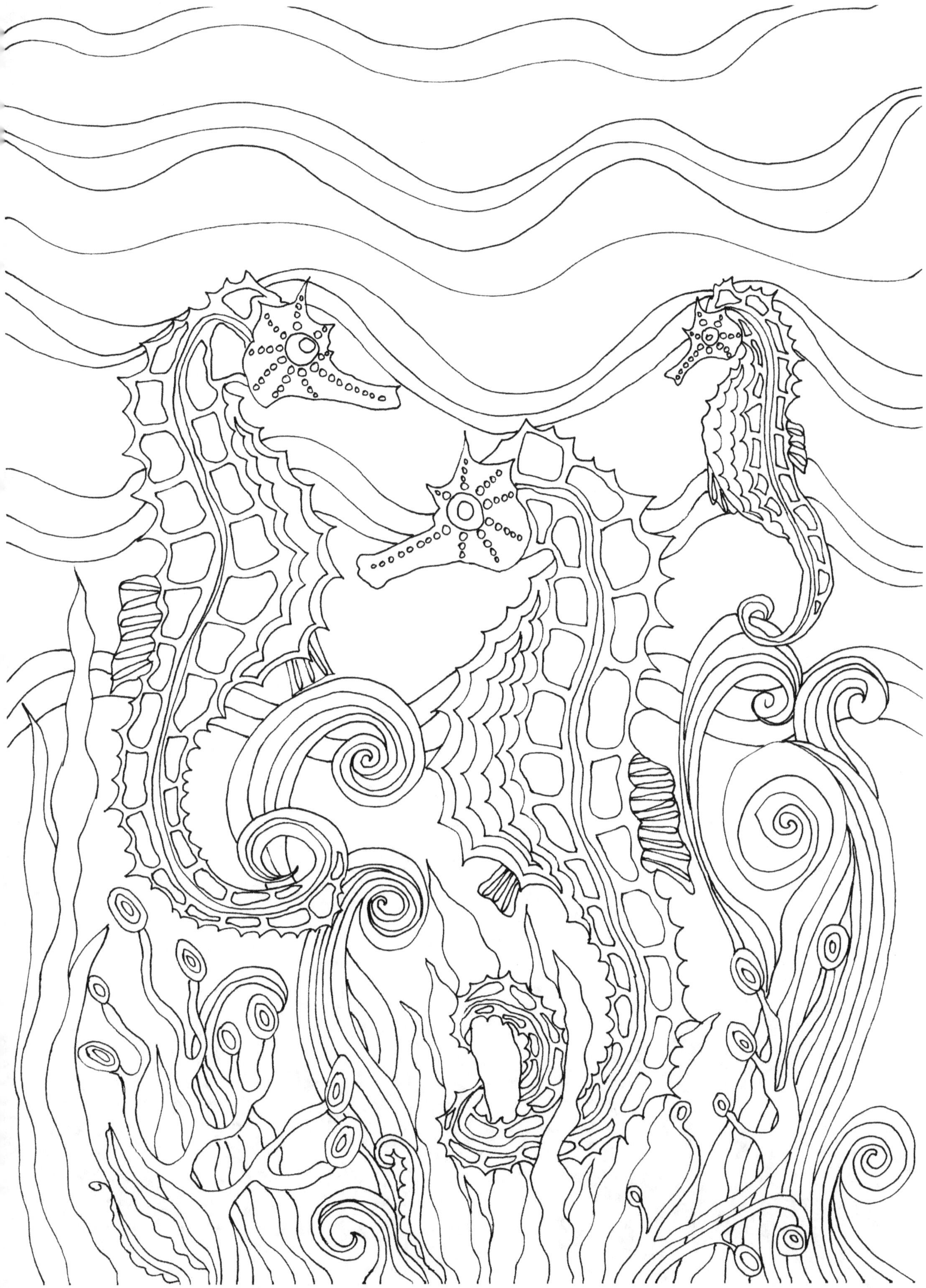

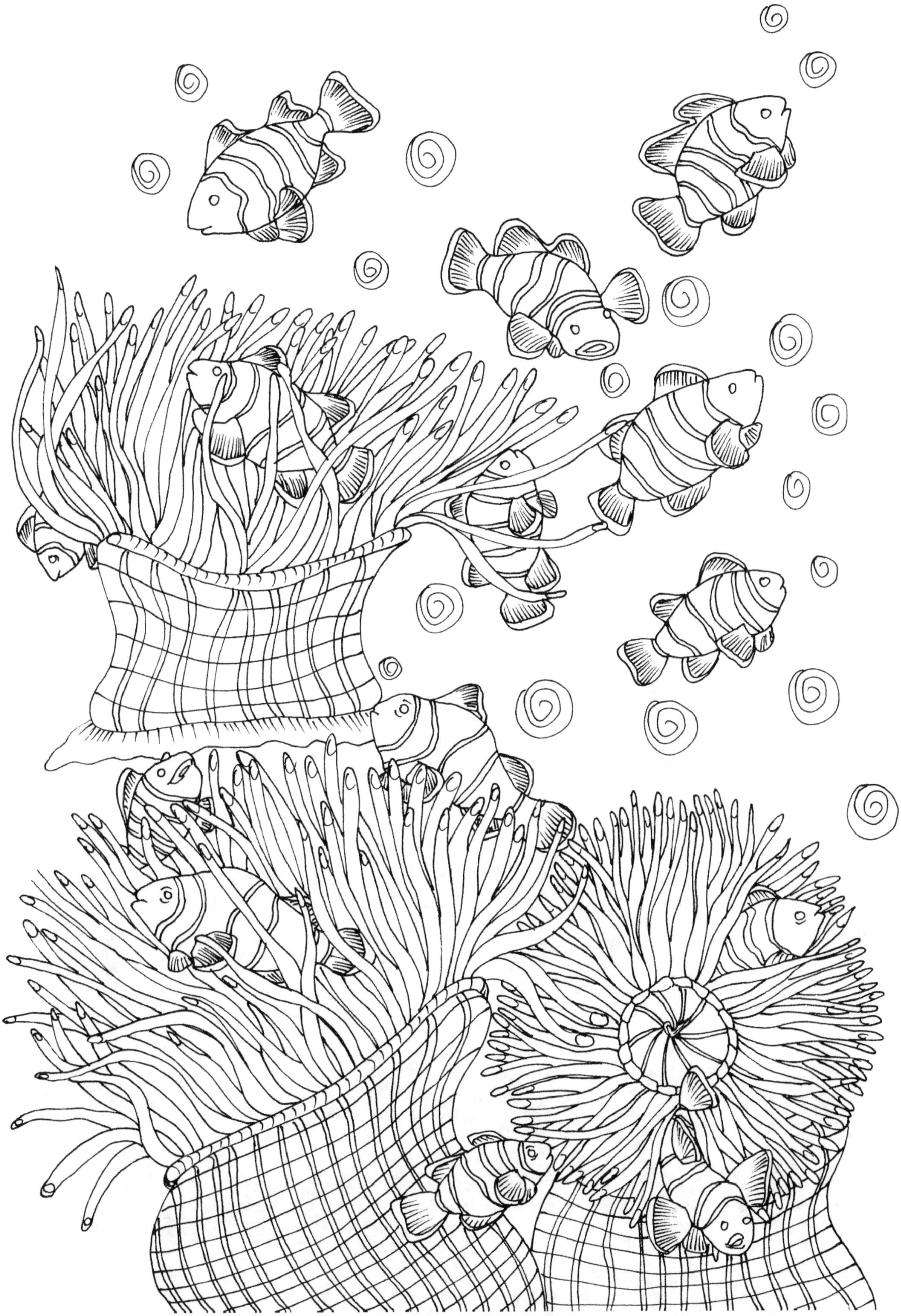

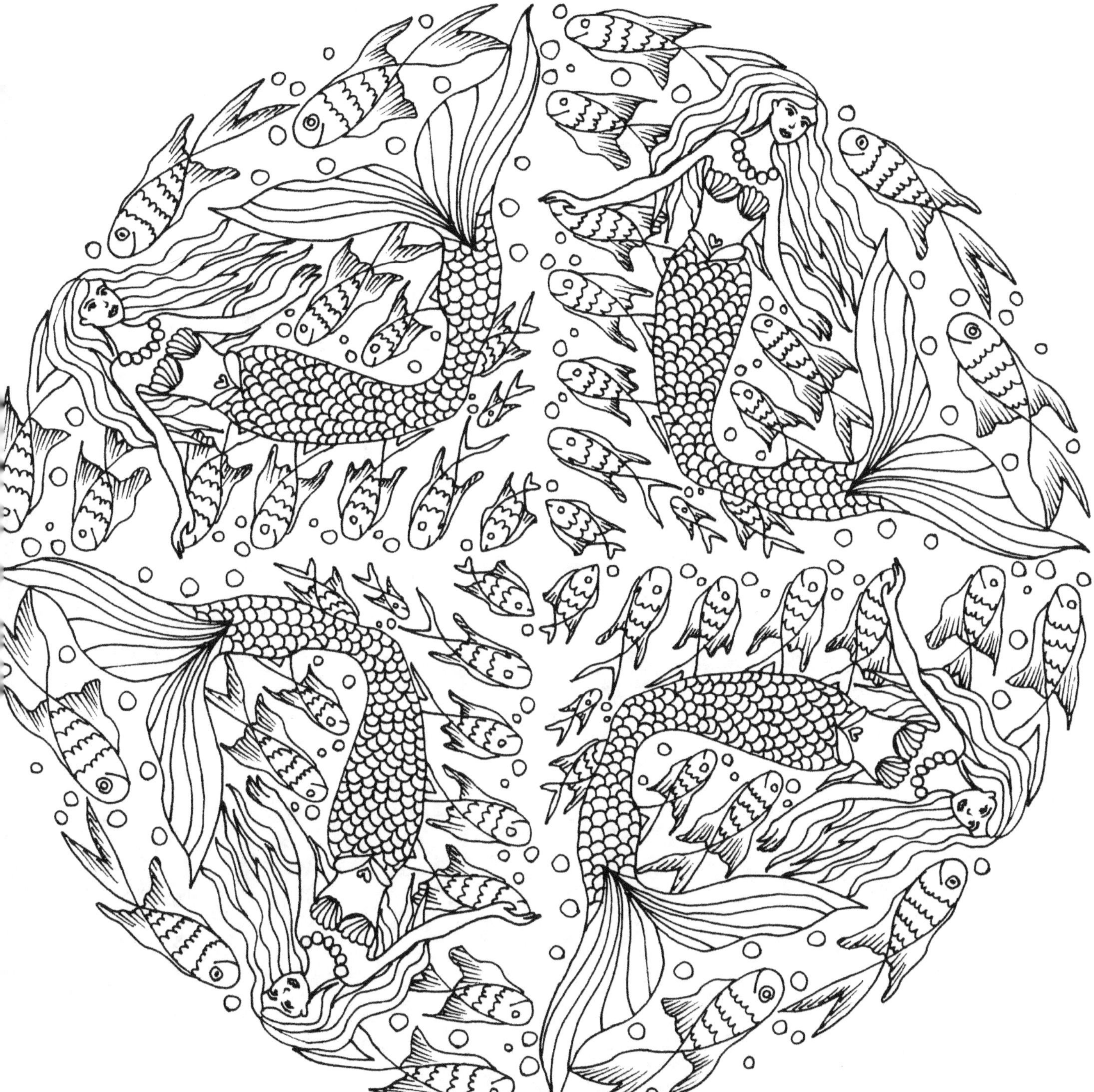

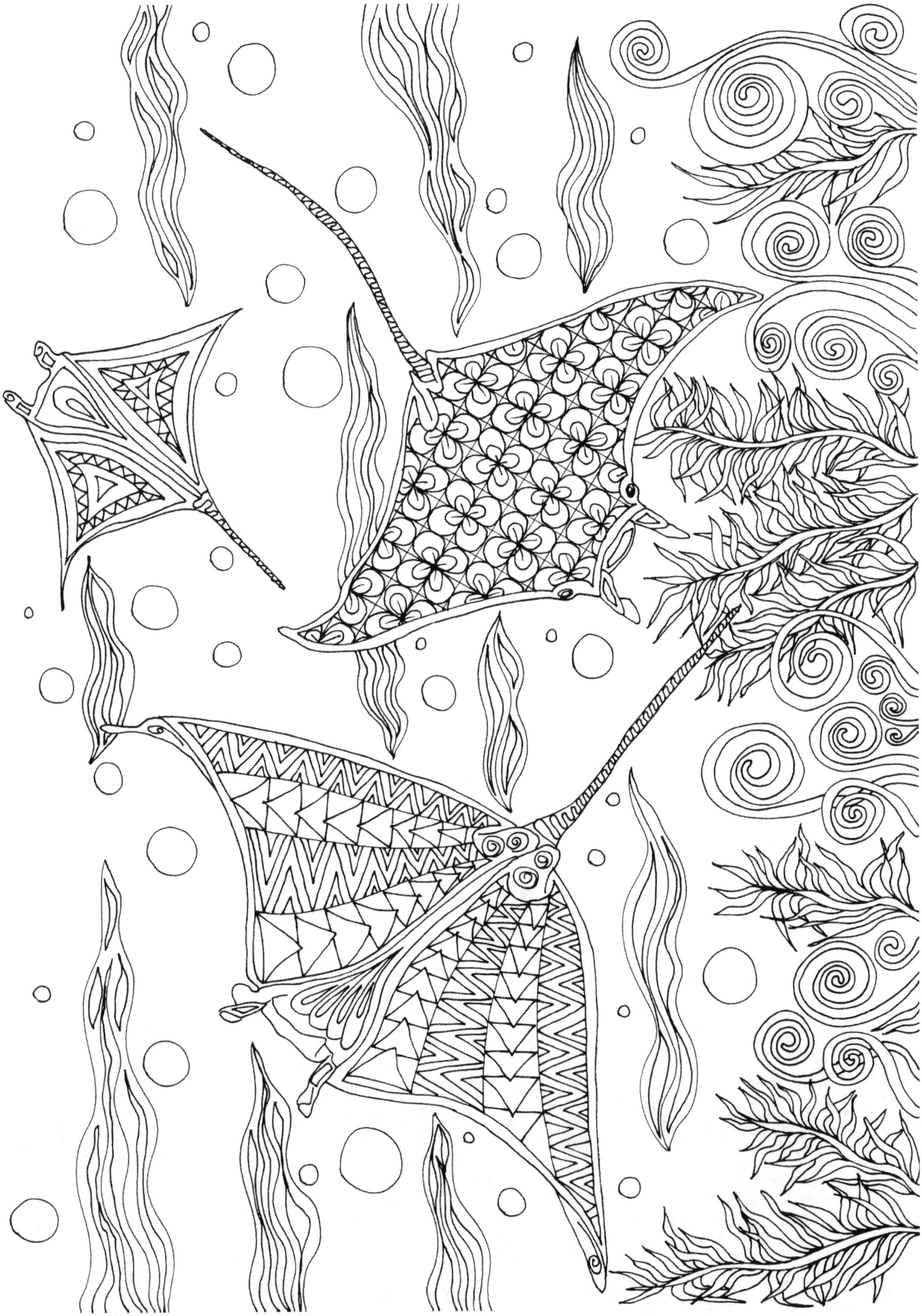

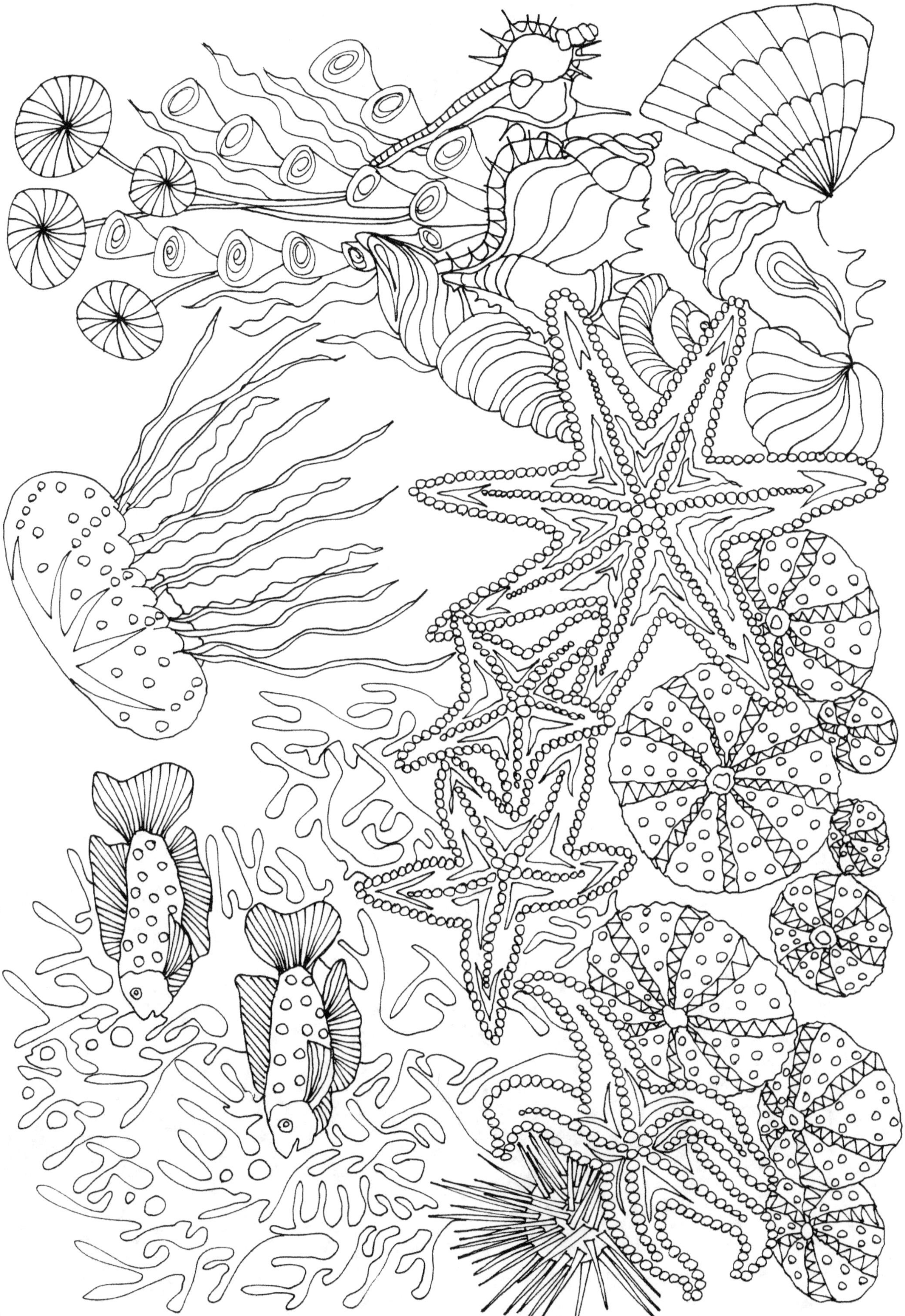

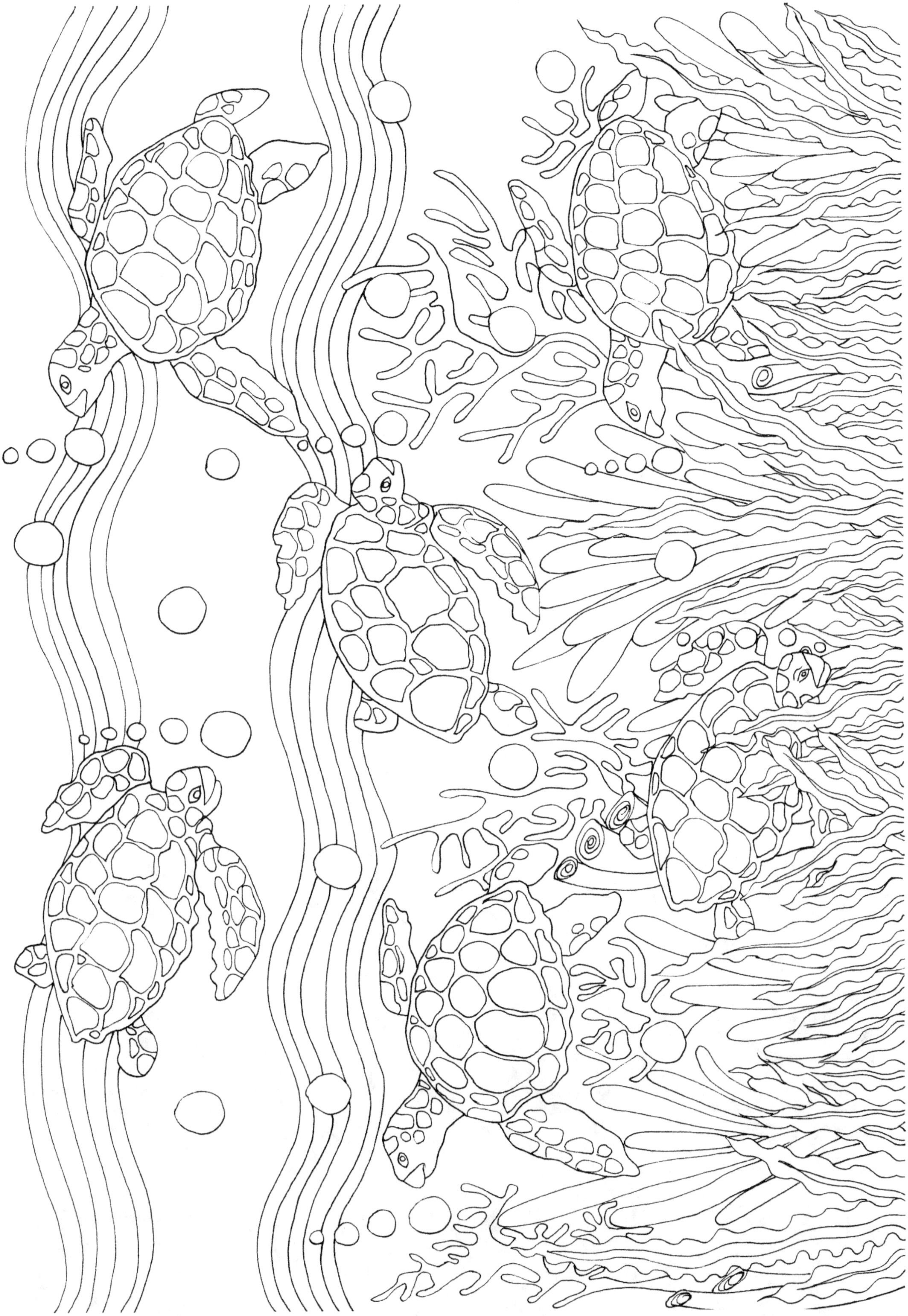

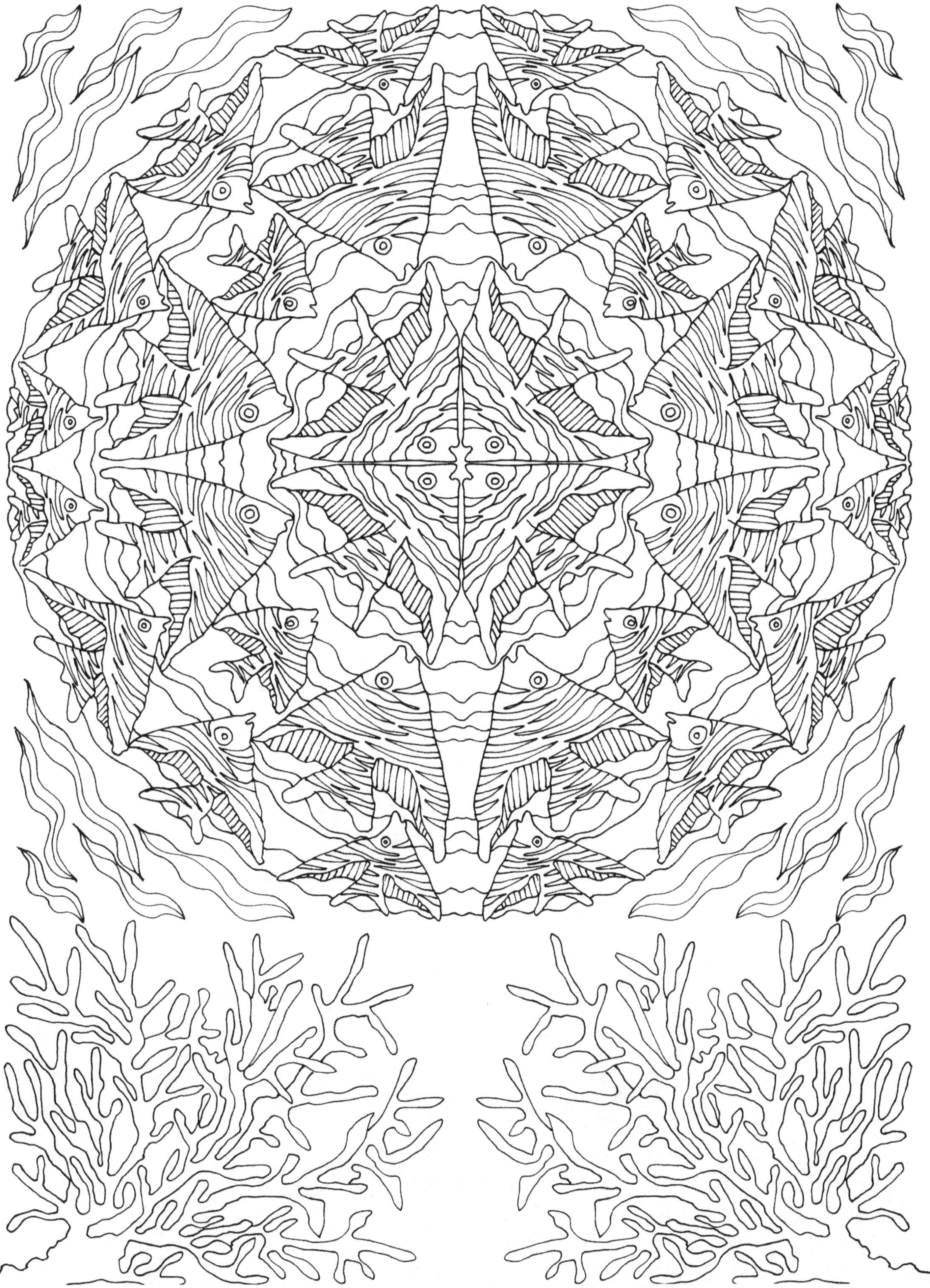

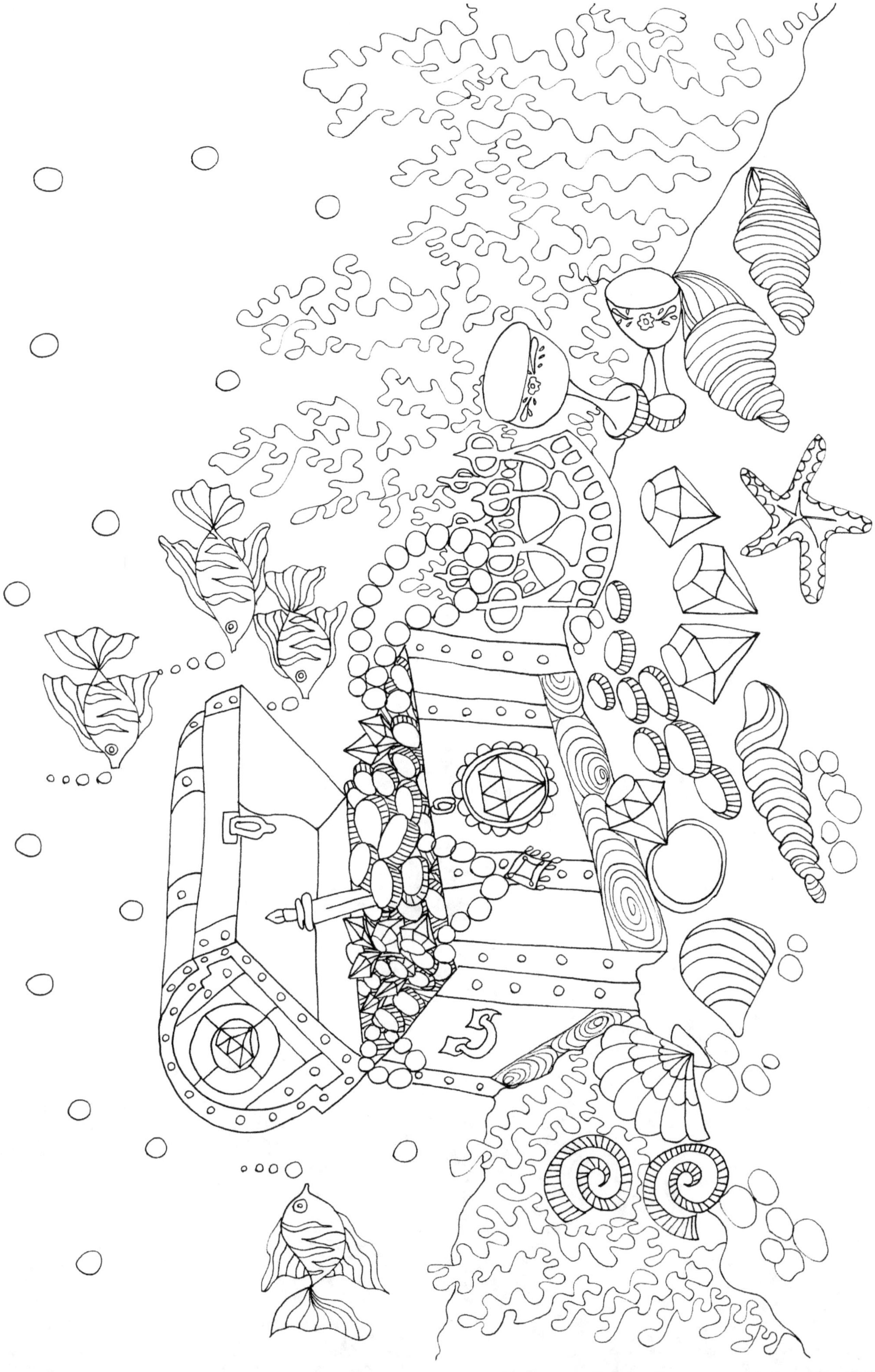

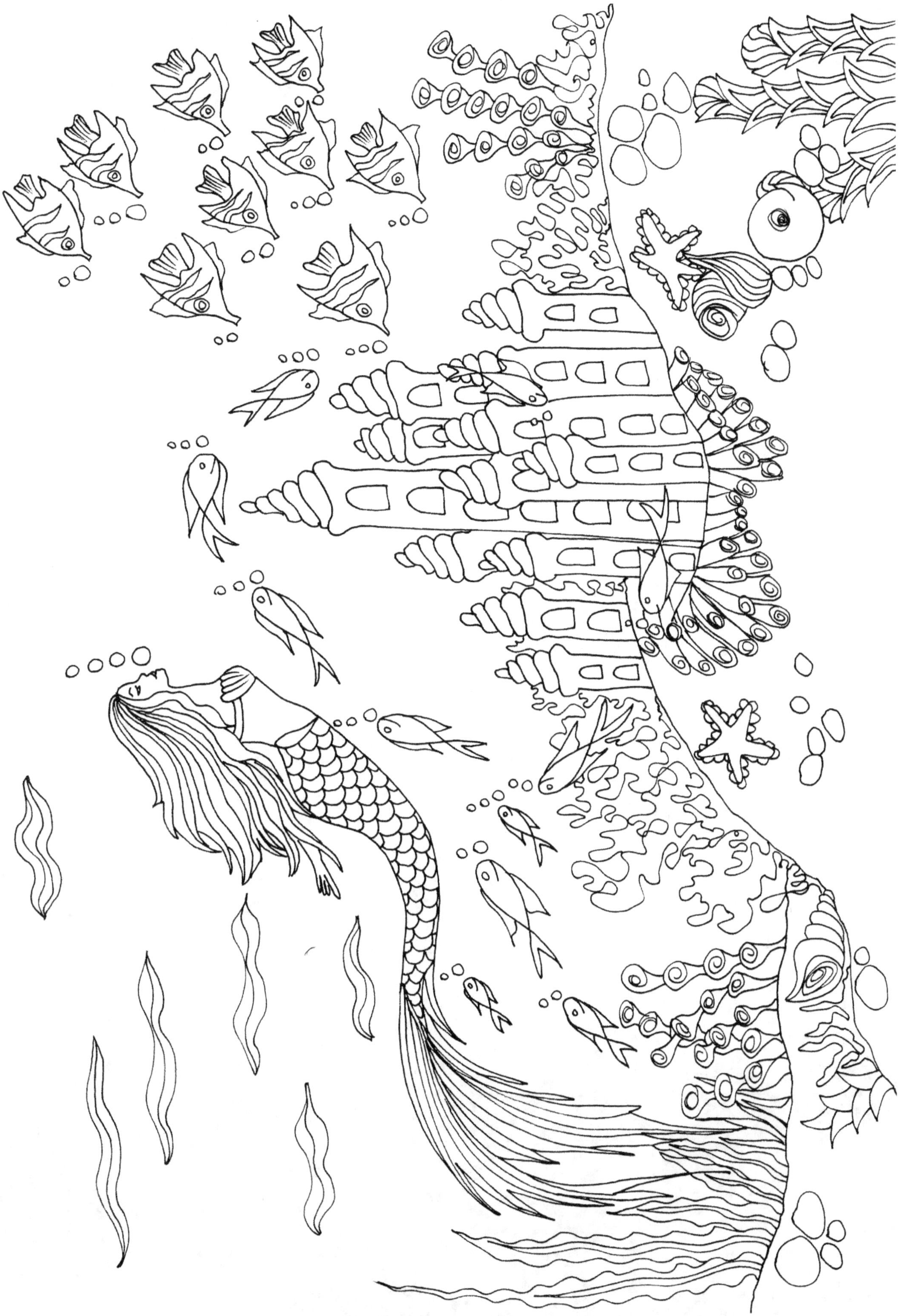

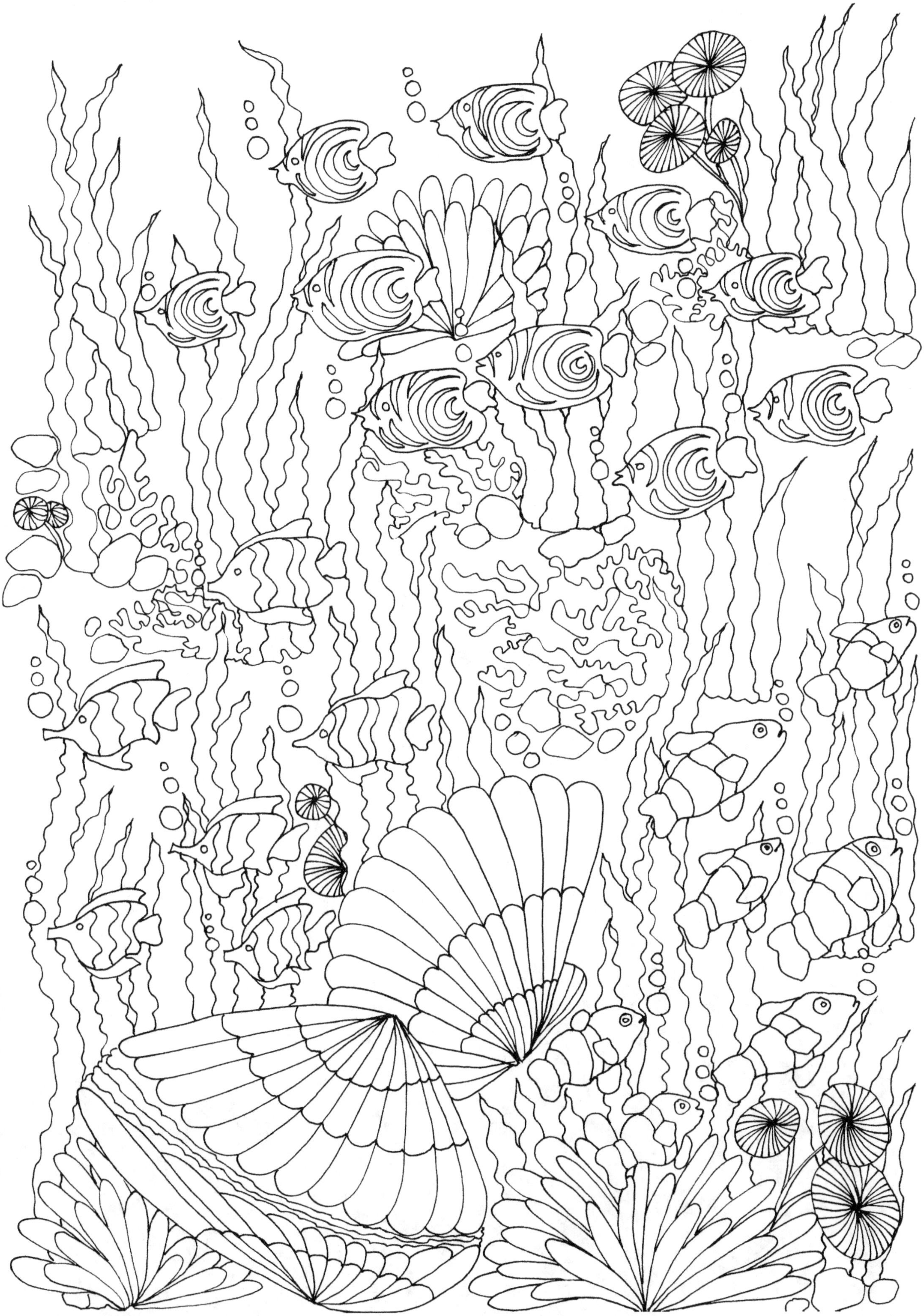

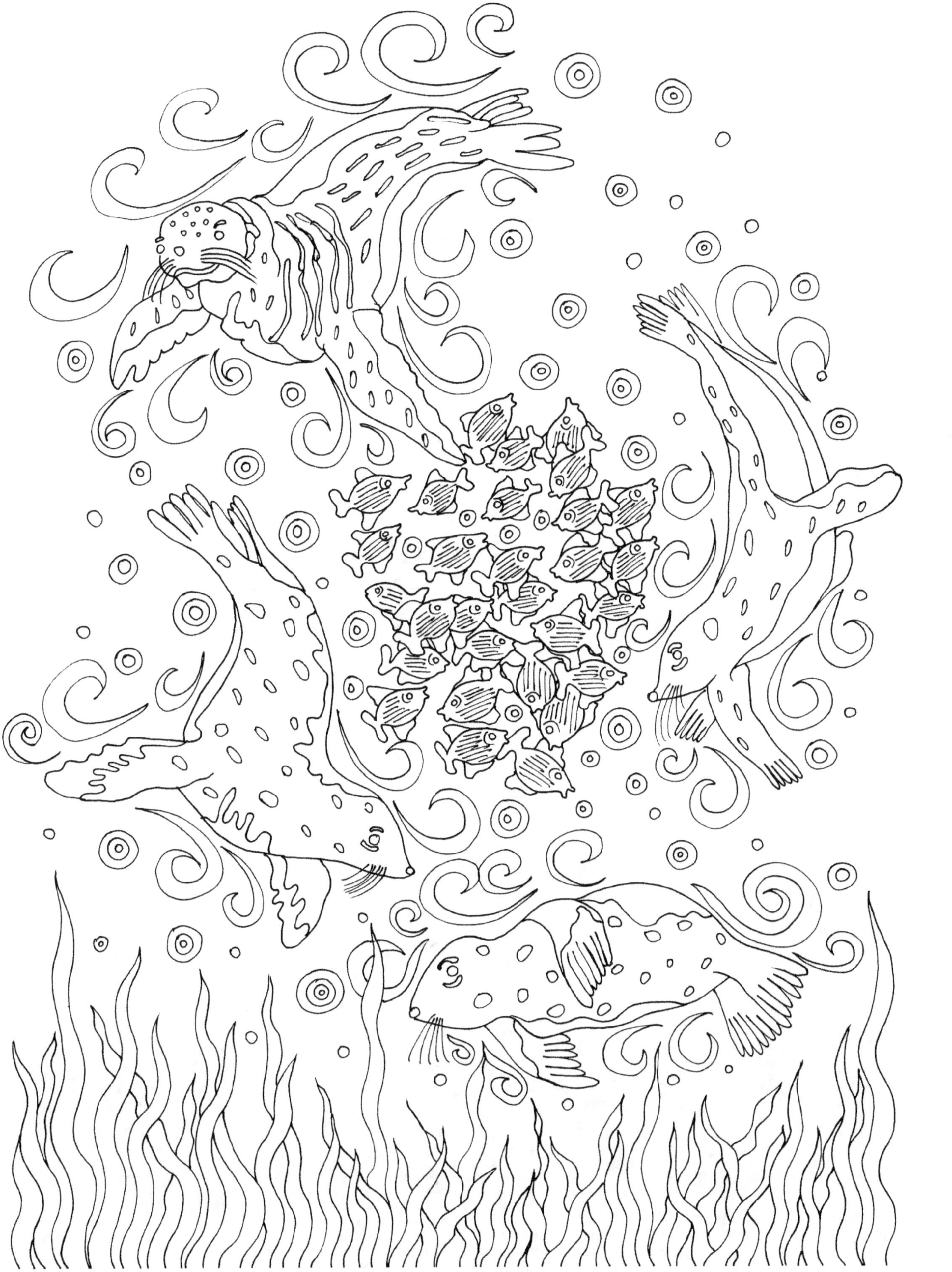

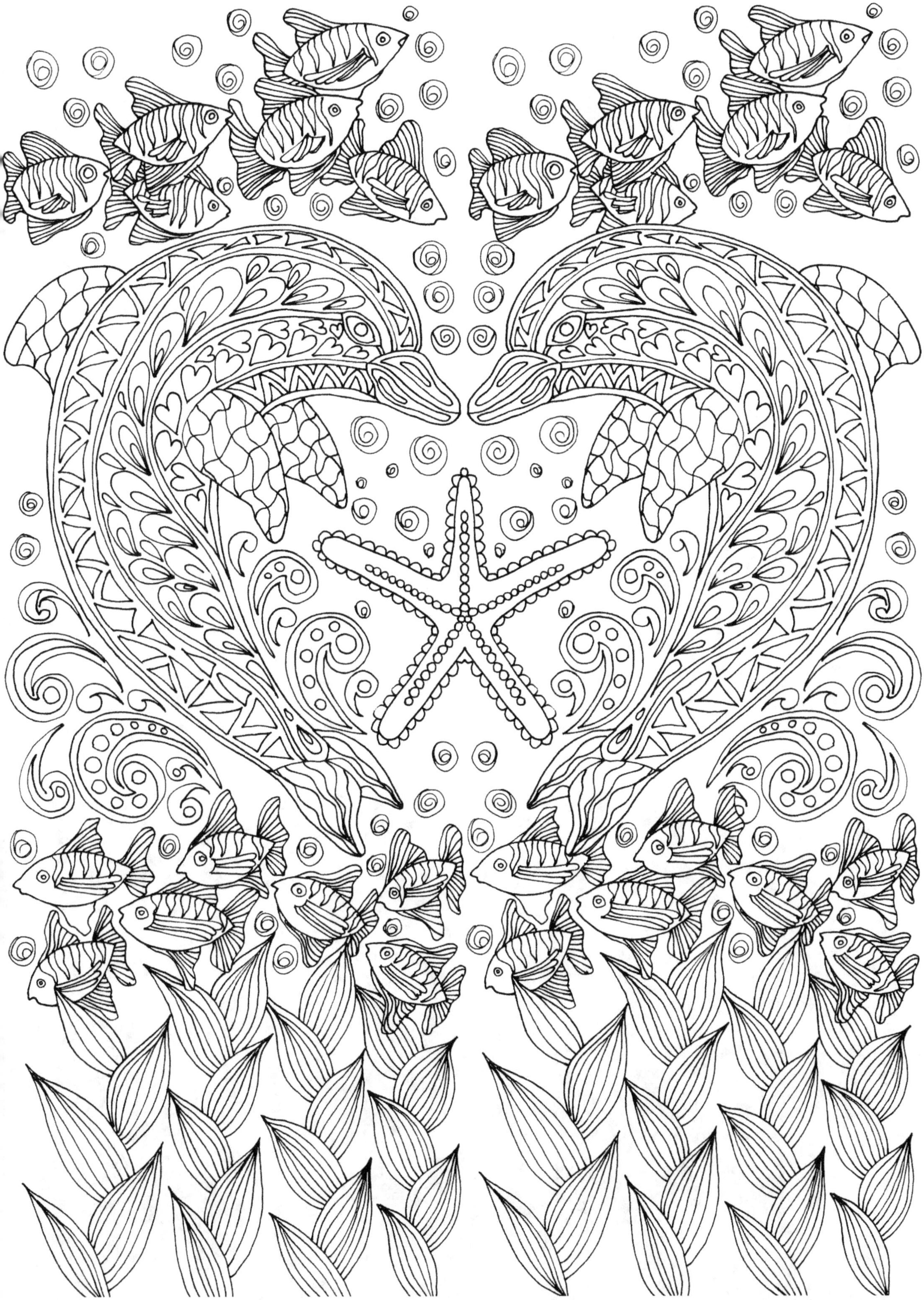

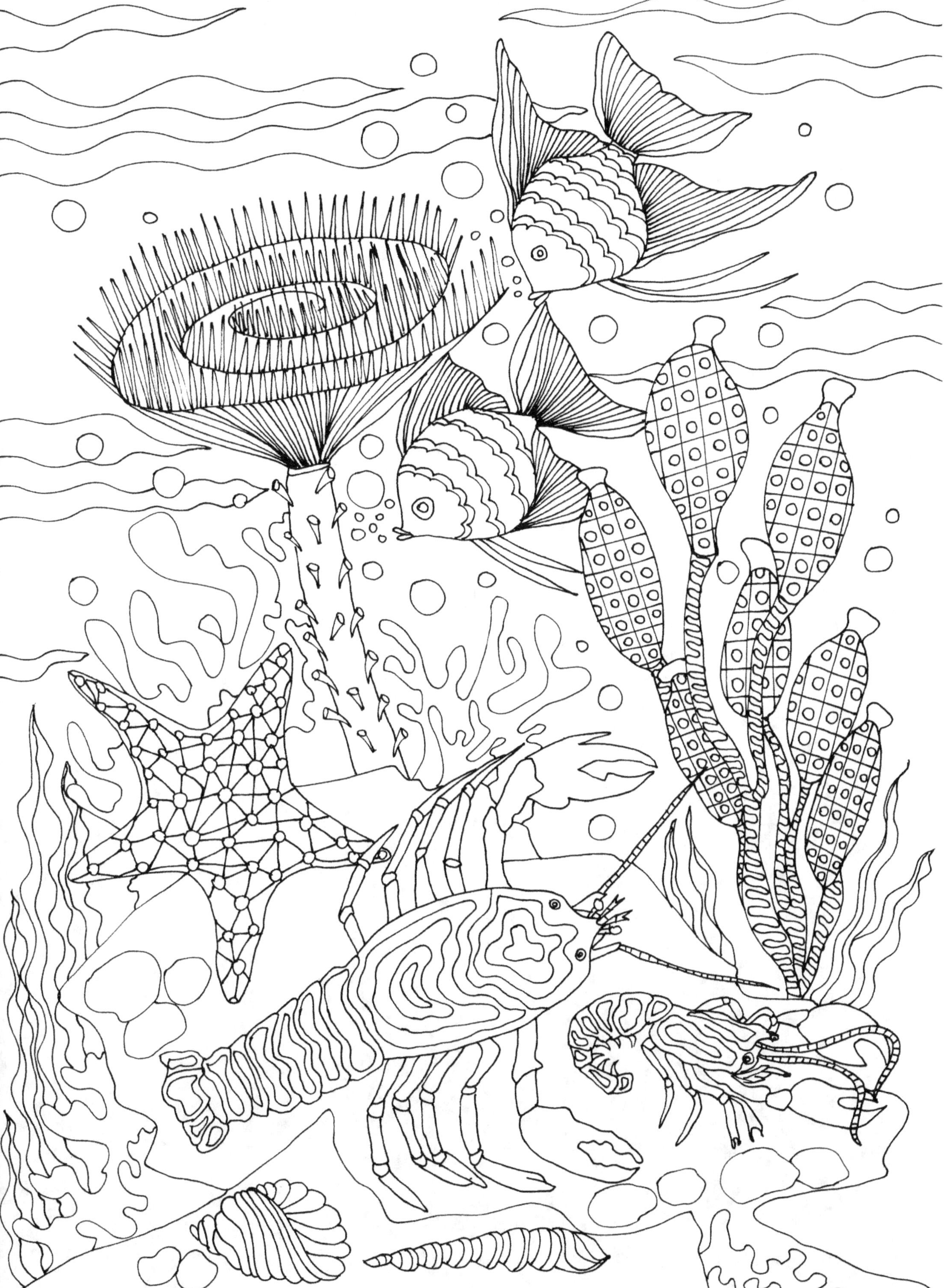

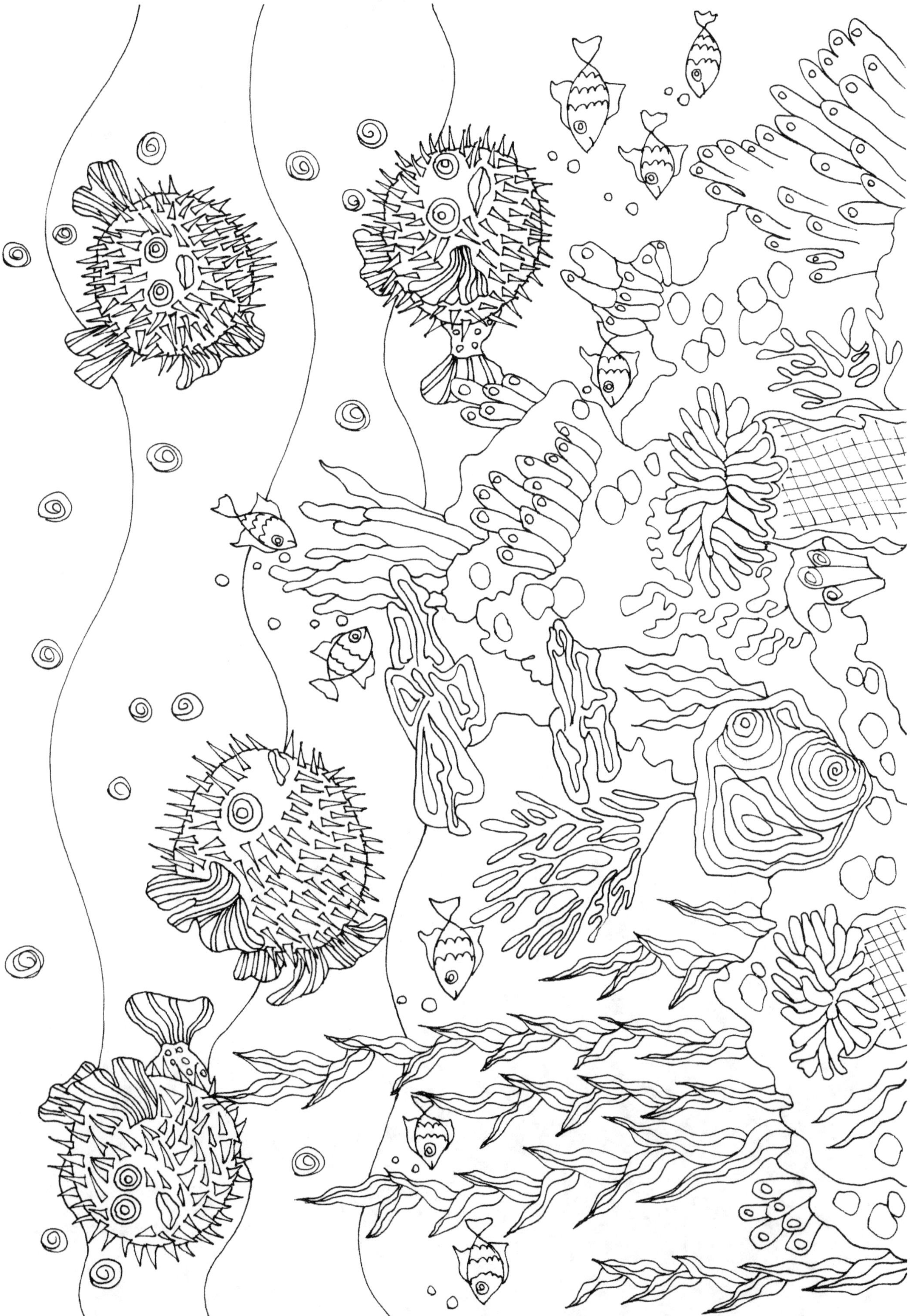

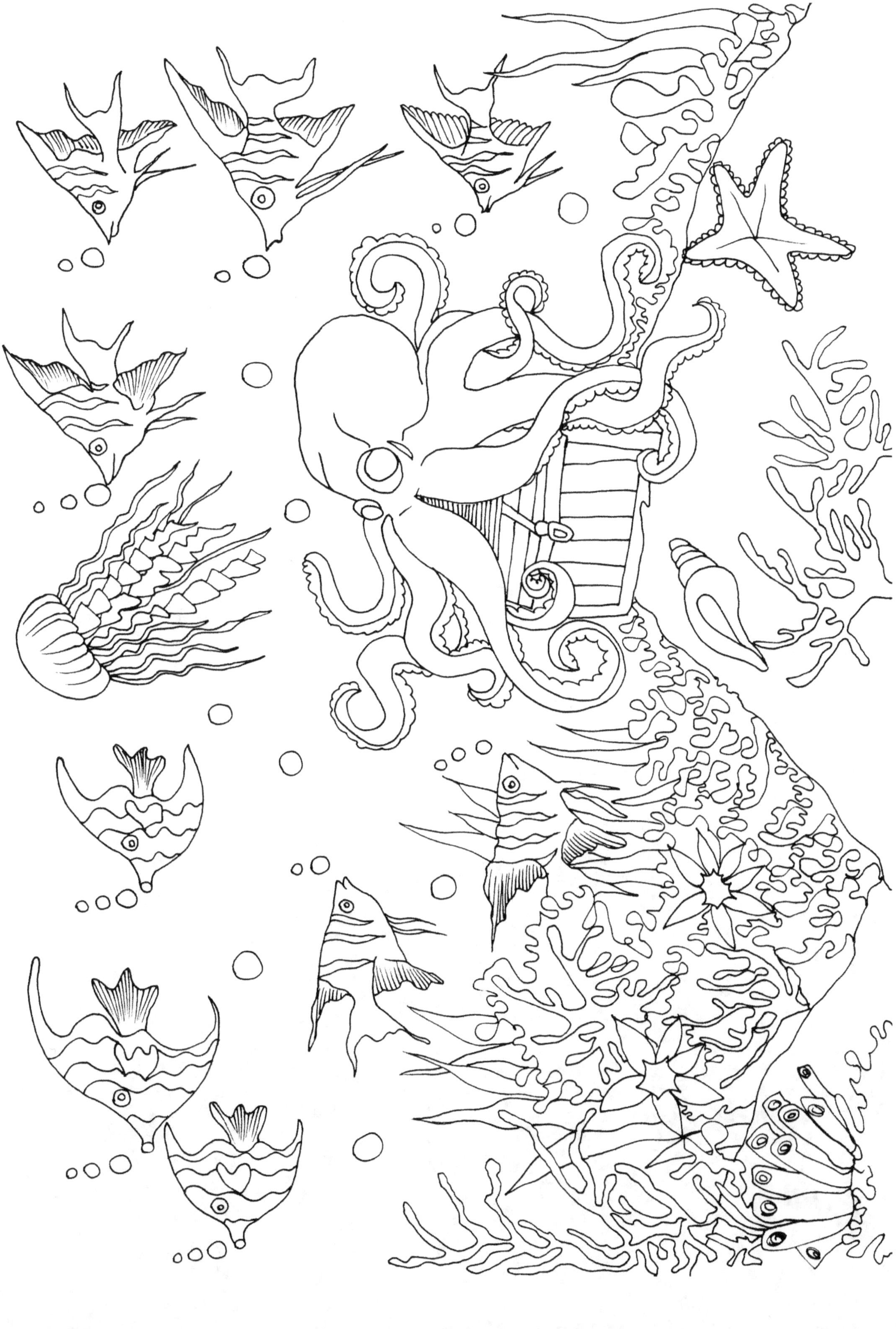

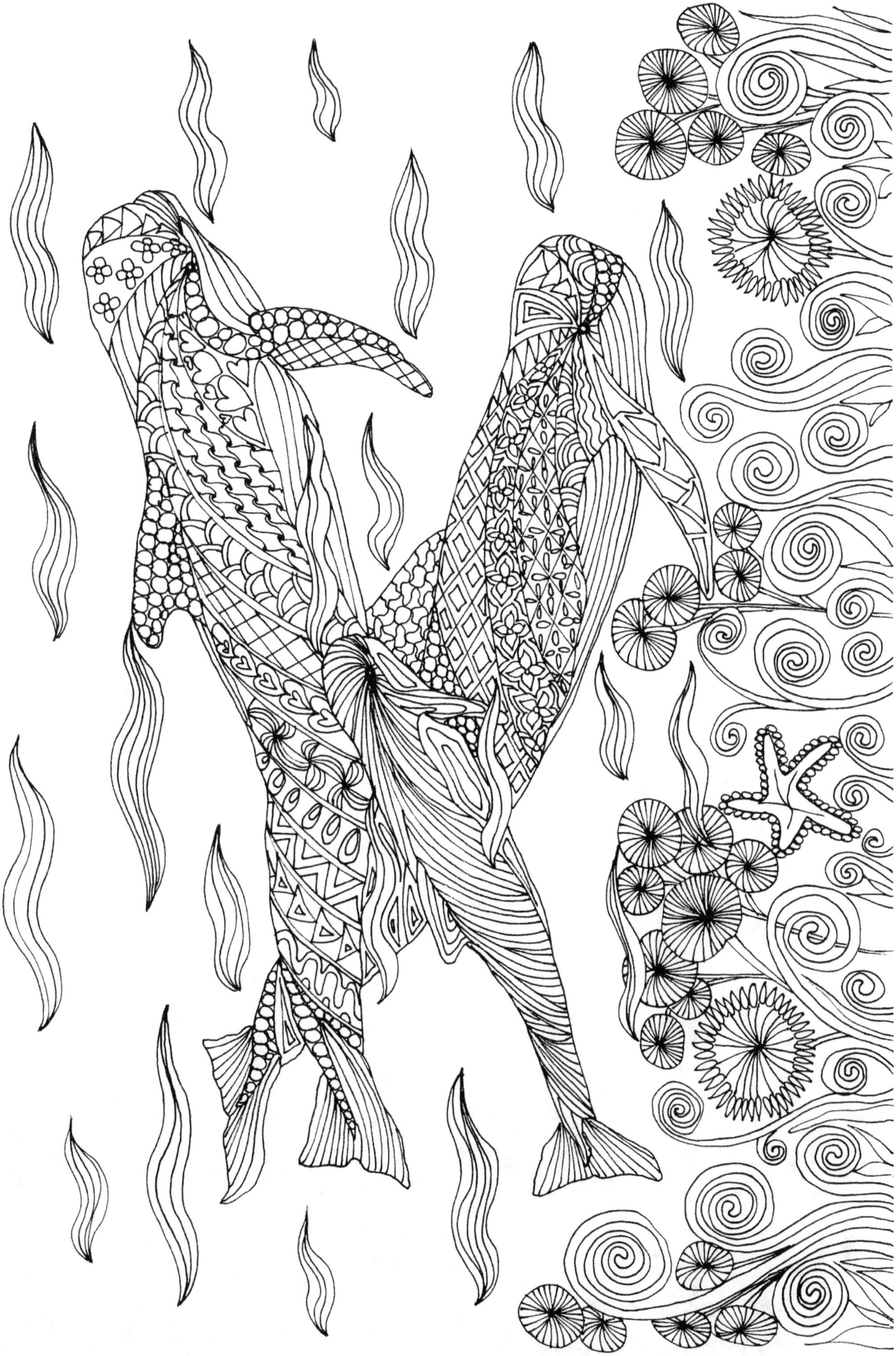

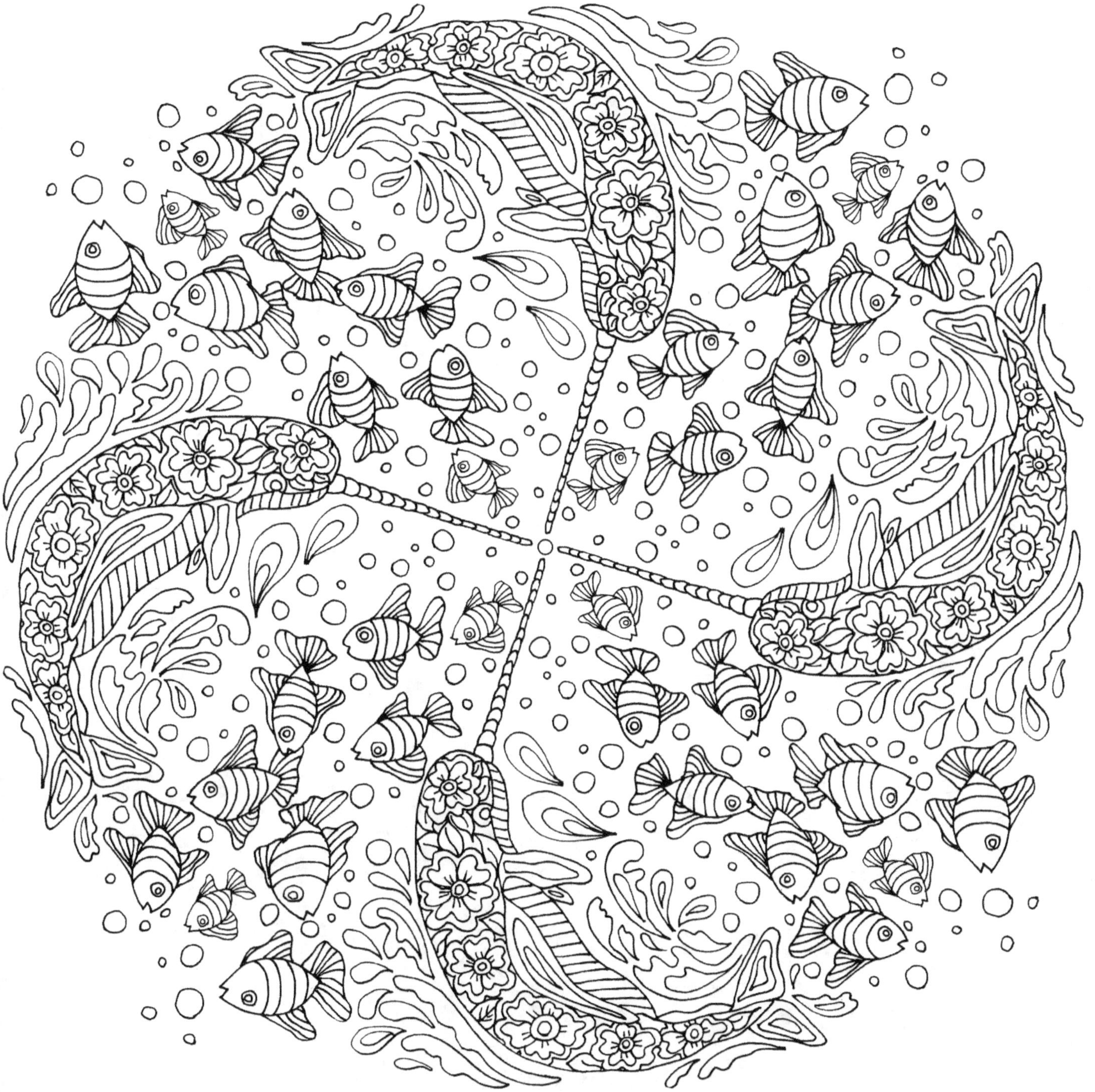

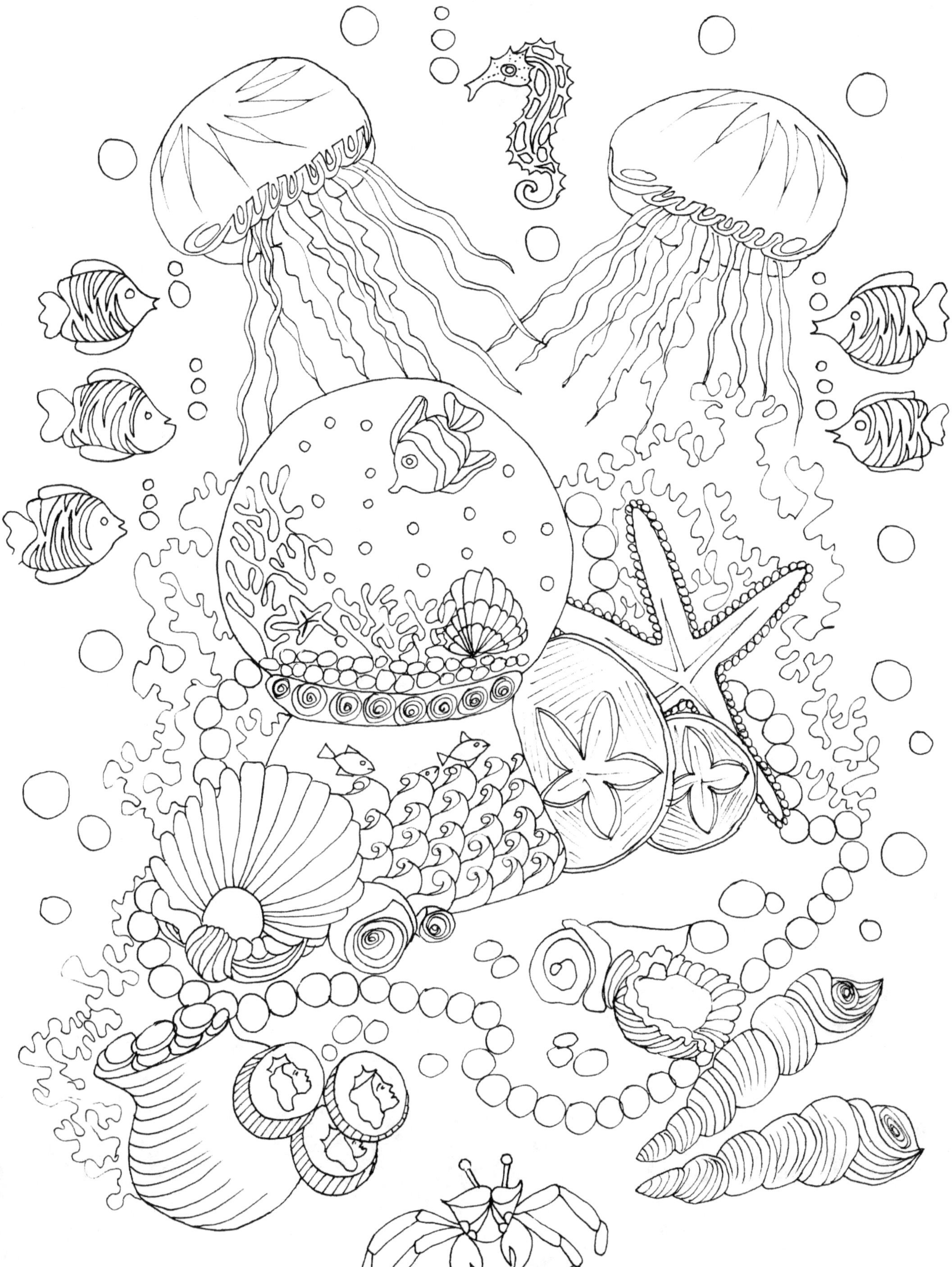

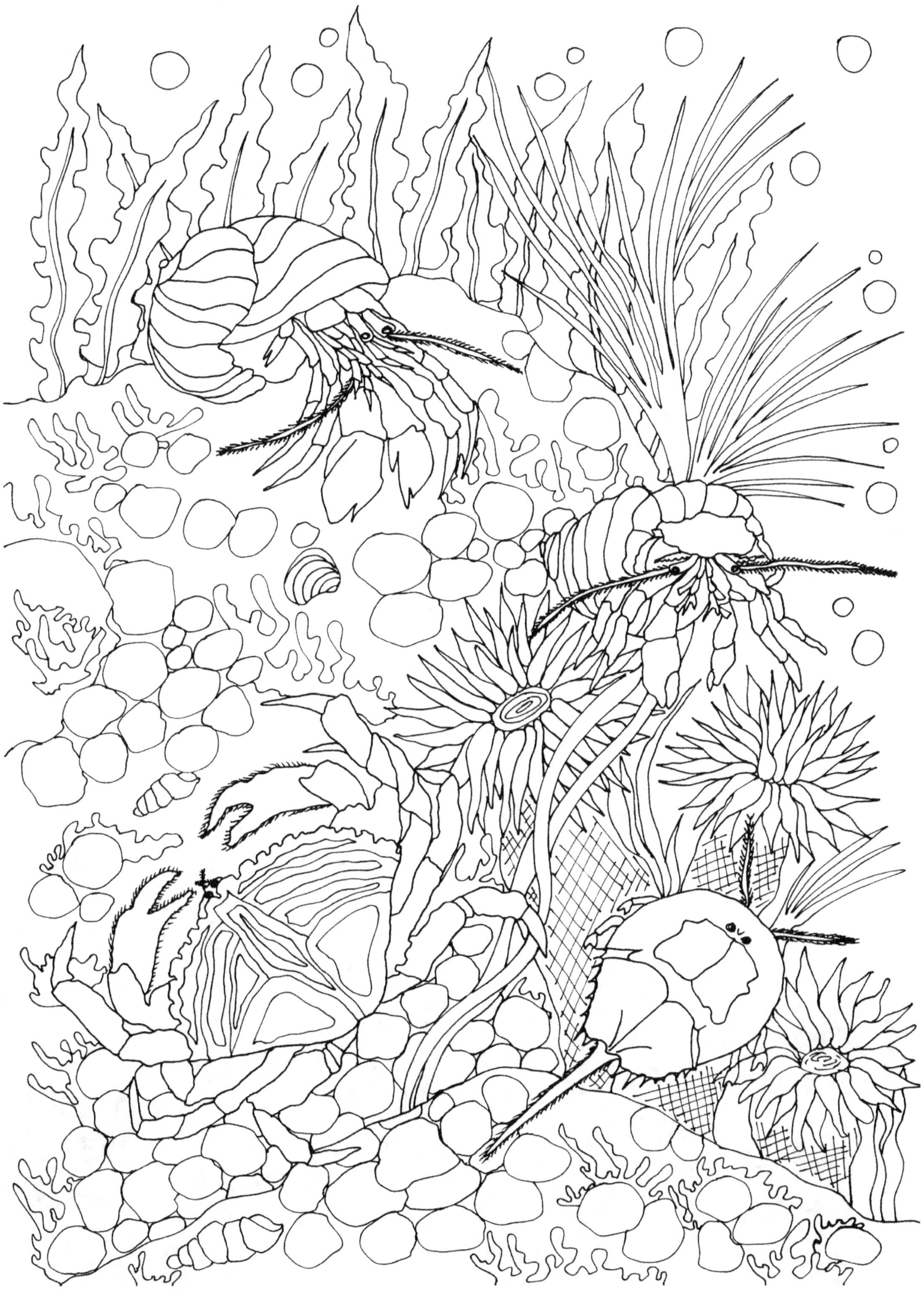

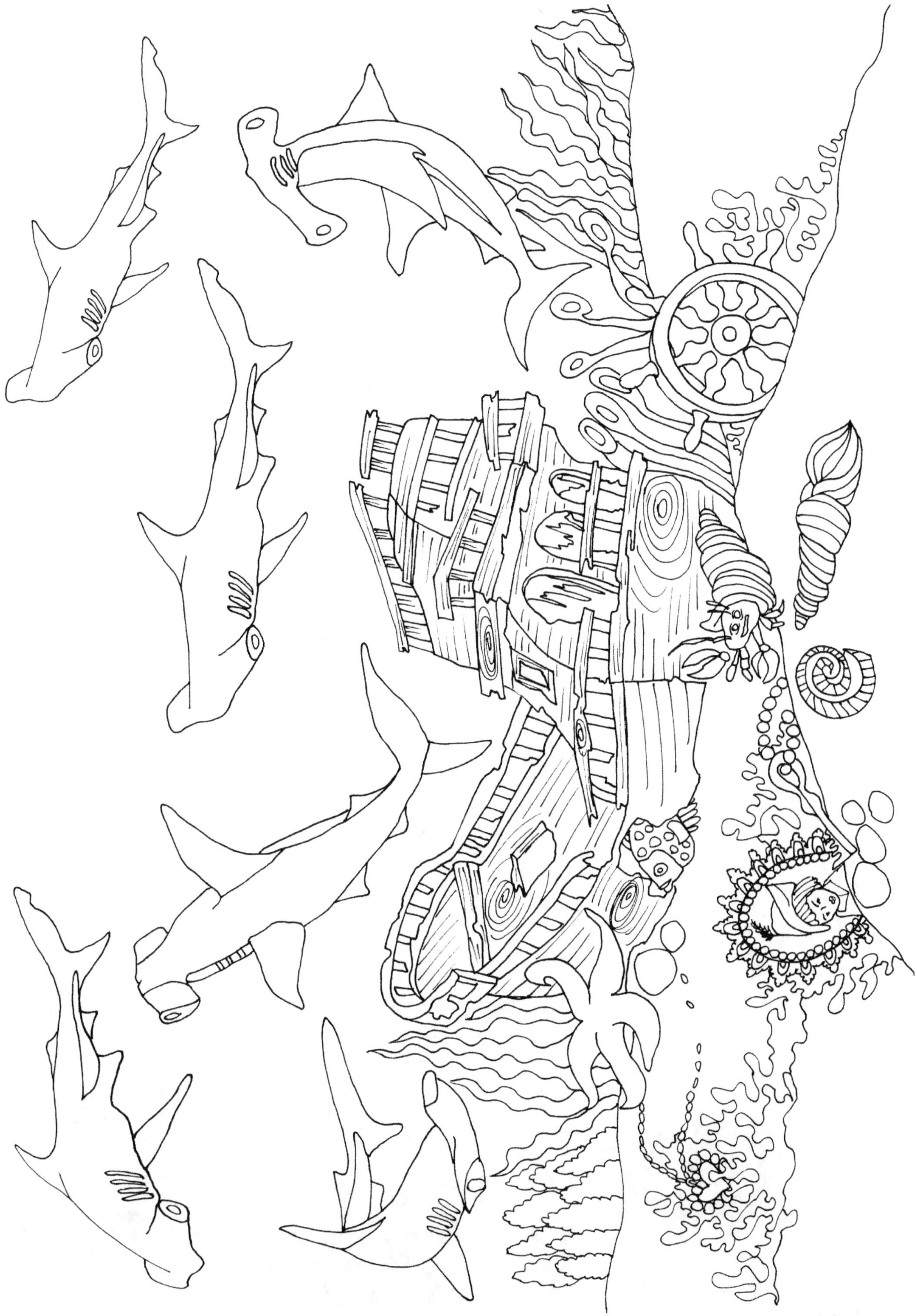

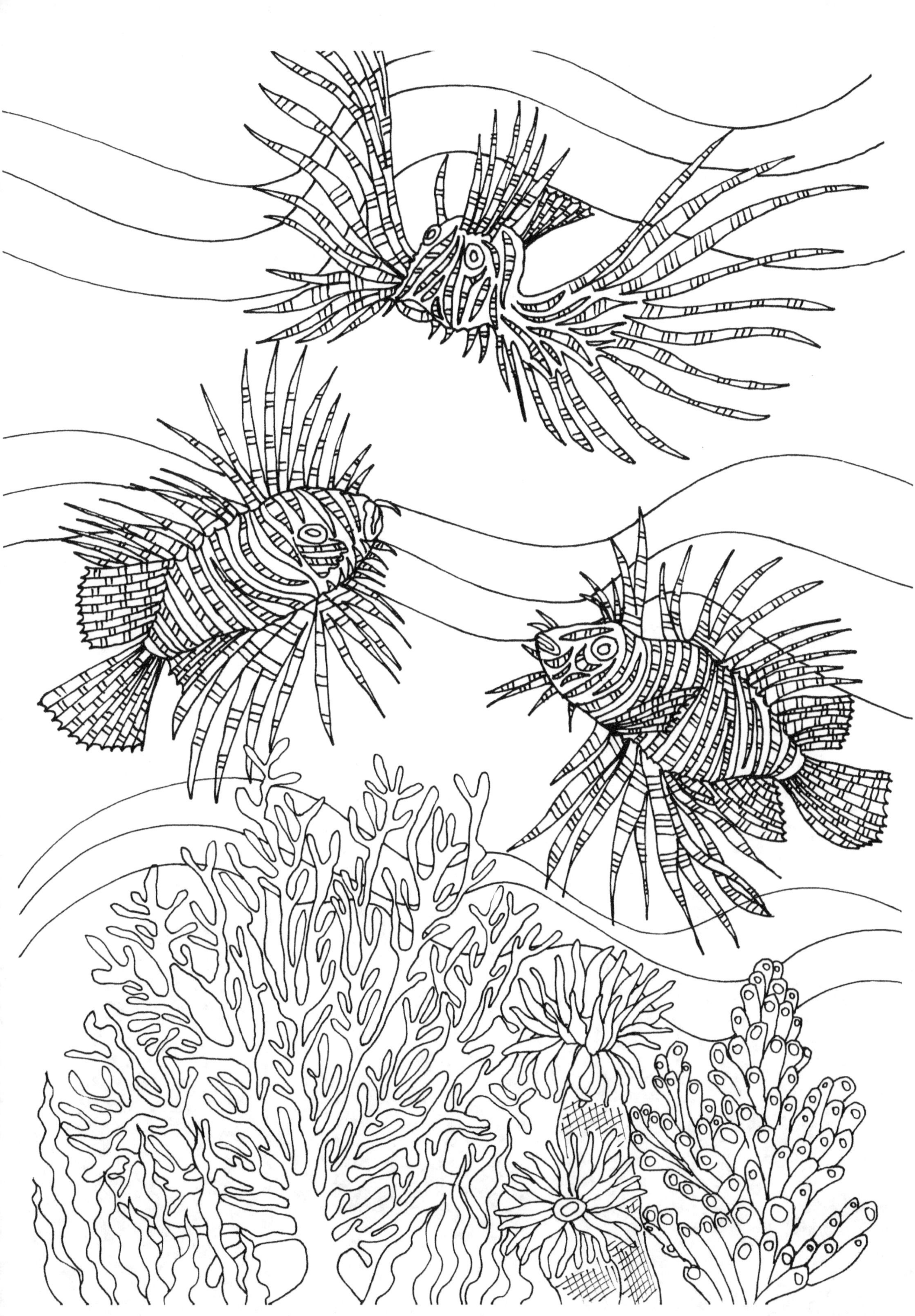

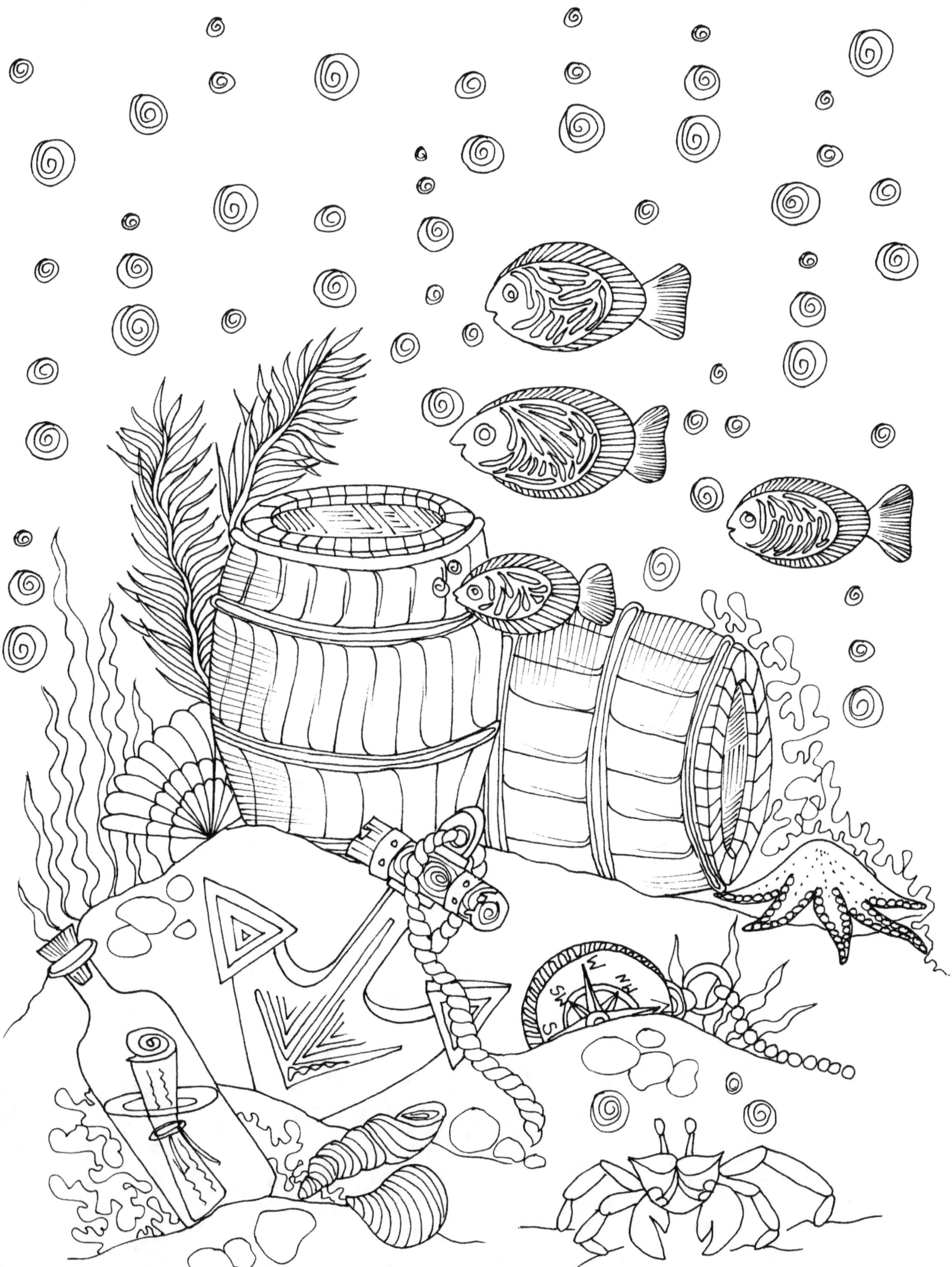

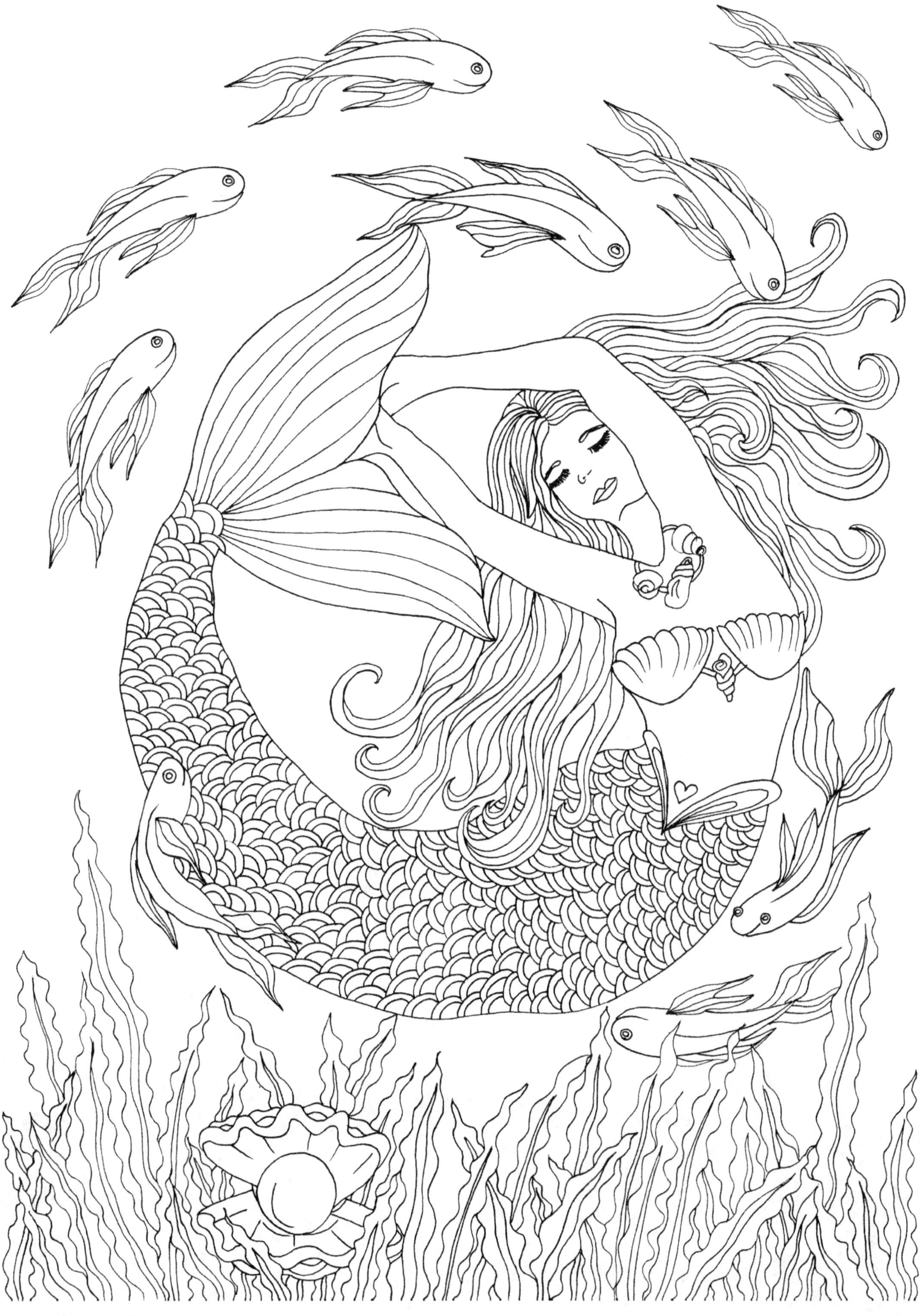

www.ingramcontent.com/pod-product-compliance
Lightning Source LLC
Chambersburg PA
CBHW080828170526
45158CB00009B/2539
* 9 7 8 0 9 9 7 0 2 9 6 2 8 *